Black Legacies

UNIVERSITY PRESS OF FLORIDA

Florida A&M University, Tallahassee
Florida Atlantic University, Boca Raton
Florida Gulf Coast University, Ft. Myers
Florida International University, Miami
Florida State University, Tallahassee
New College of Florida, Sarasota
University of Central Florida, Orlando
University of Florida, Gainesville
University of North Florida, Jacksonville
University of South Florida, Tampa
University of West Florida, Pensacola

𝕭𝖑𝖆𝖈𝖐 𝕷𝖊𝖌𝖆𝖈𝖎𝖊𝖘

Race and the European Middle Ages

Lynn T. Ramey

UNIVERSITY PRESS OF FLORIDA

Gainesville / Tallahassee / Tampa / Boca Raton

Pensacola / Orlando / Miami / Jacksonville / Ft. Myers / Sarasota

This book may be available in an electronic edition.

21 20 19 18 17 16   6 5 4 3 2 1

First cloth printing, 2014
First paperback printing, 2016

Library of Congress Control Number: 2014937644
ISBN 978-0-8130-6007-1 (cloth)
ISBN 978-0-8130-6207-5 (pbk.)

The University Press of Florida is the scholarly publishing agency for the State University System of Florida, comprising Florida A&M University, Florida Atlantic University, Florida Gulf Coast University, Florida International University, Florida State University, New College of Florida, University of Central Florida, University of Florida, University of North Florida, University of South Florida, and University of West Florida.

University Press of Florida
15 Northwest 15th Street
Gainesville, FL 32611-2079
http: / / www.upf.com

For Dwayne, Caitlyn, and Clayton

ॐ

Contents

Figures

Acknowledgments

This book has benefited from the advice, feedback, and encouragement of many, especially my colleague Holly Tucker, who was a consistent source of inspiration. Colleagues Joel Harrington and Leah Marcus read my work early on and had excellent suggestions. Two groups were seminal in this work: the Robert Penn Warren Fellows group at Vanderbilt University on premodern race in 2005–6, and an NEH seminar directed by George Hoffmann and Carla Zecher on early modern travel writing in 2005. My fellow participants in those groups lent excitement and direction to this project. Sahar Amer and Geraldine Heng provided venues for me to share earlier versions of this work and gave me their own input, always insightful. My writing groups and my research assistants Rachel Early, Chad Simpson, Megan Russell, and Sarah Kiningham gave me much-needed support. Readers and interlocutors through the years have helped me formulate my arguments: Robert Barsky, Sara Figal, Jerold Frakes, Nickolas Haydock, Sharon Kinoshita, Peggy McCracken, Joan McRae, Tison Pugh, and especially Pamela Toler. The input of anonymous reviewers from the University Press of Florida was crucial. My work grew immensely from their critiques, and I appreciate their guidance. Finally, the ILL staff and librarian Yvonne Boyer at Vanderbilt always went the extra mile to get the research materials I needed.

Early versions of parts of chapters 3, 4, and 5 appeared in the following publications, and I am grateful for permission to reuse the material: "Monstrous Alterity in Early Modern Travel Accounts: Lessons from the Ambiguous Medieval Discourse on Humanness," *Esprit Créateur* 48.1 (2008): 81–95; "Medieval Miscegenation: Hybridity and the Anxiety of Inheritance," in *Contextualizing the Muslim Other in Medieval Judeo-*

Christian Discourses, ed. Jerold Frakes (New York: Palgrave, 2011), 1–19; "'La geste que Turoldus declinet': History and Authorship in Frank Cassenti's *Chanson de Roland* (France, 1978)," in *Hollywood in the Holy Land: The Fearful Symmetries of Movie Medievalism*, ed. Nickolas Haydock and Edward Risden (Jefferson, N.C.: McFarland, 2009), 147–60.

Introduction

This book is primarily focused on the legacy of the Middle Ages to the development of racial prejudice and ultimately black-white problems in the West. From the outset, I wish to underscore that this book examines the question of color and (premodern) genetics as applied eventually to persons of color. I look at racism in its incarnation as a form of xenophobia, directed toward the unknown person or culture. This book does not have as a primary goal the treatment of racism directed against Jews for several reasons, the first being that there are several good studies on medieval anti-Semitism already in circulation and others under preparation.[1] Secondly, European Jews, though certainly viewed as outside the Christian societal core, lived and worked within Western culture, with and beside dominant cultures. The interest in medieval anti-Semitism is well justified, but the color question is an equally intriguing one and deserves, I think, some discussion on its own. This is not to minimize the racism directed toward medieval Jews, but rather to explore a different type and manifestation of racism. While the role of other forms of prejudice—anti-Semitism, xenophobia, misogyny—will be discussed as they relate to the question of color, the main focus of the book will intentionally remain that of color. My attention is directed toward prejudice against darker-skinned persons from non-Western cultures precisely because of their skin color and their usually imagined, always unfamiliar, cultural practices.

My interest grew out of my earlier study of cultural interactions between Christians and Muslims in medieval French literature and history.[2] The representations of "Saracen" characters in medieval French literature were so many and varied that it made me wonder what impact these images had on subsequent views of the foreign Other; are Western views of Islam or Muslims today in any way shaped by the medieval past? Written in the shadow of Said's *Orientalism* and studies that refined and questioned his view of the role of the Arab in Western culture, my book focused on the medieval discourse about the conflict and desire that arose from contact between Arabs and Christians, beginning with the Islamic invasions of the eighth century and culminating in the Crusades that dominated the medieval period. My goal then was to show how the rubbing together of these two cultures produced a dynamic that was essential to the development of French identity and major medieval literary themes and genres. Now I aim to look at the legacy of this central element of the medieval period in later aspects of European civilization, namely the formulation of a racial consciousness. Can we see elements of what medieval writers, thinkers, and artists produced in racial discourses in the West today? What other thoughts were in those conversations in the past, ideas that did not make it to the present? What might it have been like to describe a proto-racial society?[3]

Despite widespread belief that race is a uniquely modern construct, many elements of the key discourses on race were already present in the Middle Ages. Climate-based theories that black skin develops from the heat of the sun were well articulated long before the fourteenth century. Literature of the twelfth and thirteenth centuries already shows a preoccupation with skin color and the coding of black as evil and white as good. Law codes of fifteenth-century Spain exhibit a preoccupation with "purity of blood," and literary works from Germany and France indicate that despite conversion a trace, or taint, of infidel blood could remain and preclude complete integration. All medieval European societies showed legal and literary fears of miscegenation.

Regardless of the commonalities between the medieval and the modern conception of race, this book does not claim that the two discourses are equivalent. In the medieval period there was a cacophony of discourses on what difference is and how it affects social interaction. Religion was a key part of the dialogue, and while commentaries written in the medieval period give the first hints of ways that the Christian Bible would later be used to justify slavery and racism, the idea that all Christians are part of a universal (and equal) brotherhood of believers held sway in many medieval communities.

What I hope to accomplish with this book is to bring to light some of the consistent themes surrounding race that have been present since the Middle Ages. Both medievalists and modernists could benefit from a more open-minded view of the Middle Ages that would show continuities and recognize variations rather than assuming a violent rupture between medieval and modern life and culture. Imagining the Middle Ages as a period completely free of racial consciousness not only creates an untenable and unrealistic view of the Middle Ages as a golden age of cohabitation, it also erases the history of prejudice that was present from what many consider to be the foundation of European civilization.

My work does not seek to prove that the origin of racial consciousness can be found in the Middle Ages. Other scholars have studied the antique period as well as early Jewish, Christian, and Islamic thought, often finding that the periods that they study were free from color prejudice.[4] What I find is that the key elements that form the foundations for both colonial expansion and nineteenth-century scientific racism can already be located in certain strands of medieval discourse. These strands are picked up at different points as one traces the history of racial thought. While we may never know what the average medieval person thought about people who looked or believed differently, some ideas from the Middle Ages were passed along. Thus the major objective of this study is the legacy of the medieval period in later visions of race and difference. Two moments emerge as pivotal: the European "discovery" of the New World in the sixteenth century and, equally important, the rise of scientific racism in the nineteenth century.

The construction of our vision of the Middle Ages was performed largely by Renaissance and nineteenth-century thinkers. Perhaps the first to criticize the medieval period, Petrarch lamented the disappearance of the Roman Empire and the subsequent darkness that descended upon Europe. For Petrarch and other Renaissance thinkers, it was important to define their own age against a dark past where ancient knowledge was lost, a past whose link with the Catholic Church could cast it as a monolithically unquestioning, hyper-religious society whose only focus was on the next life. Likewise, the Renaissance saw the power elite of the Middle Ages as a group that was distinctly nonreligious and that exploited the common people through their religious faith.

In the nineteenth century, particularly in France, it was this very element of religiosity that appealed to those who staged a Gothic revival.

Not that they called for a return to religious dogmatism, but the idea of a "primitive," pure culture that formed the basis for modern culture played into prevailing notions of nationalism. Much work has been done on the origins of medieval studies and the field's importance to nineteenth- and twentieth-century nationalism. What this work skirts, but does not ever directly deal with, is that the formation of systematic scientific views on race and the concomitant racism went hand in hand with notions of European nationalism in the nineteenth and twentieth centuries. In many cases where there is a call to turn to the past to recognize certain values, there is a tendency to privilege that time because of its simplicity and purity. Elements of complexity, hybridity, even exoticism in the medieval world would stand in conflict with this vision of the past.

My own study begins in chapter 1 with a foray into the nineteenth century, the period in which the Middle Ages became a field of academic study. From the outset we can see that even the first medievalists struggled with questions of race and the Middle Ages, and their practices shaped our very notions of the medieval past. The nineteenth century, a key era in the history of racial thought in the West, was preoccupied with finding scientific rules and methods to describe virtually everything, racial difference very much included. In nineteenth-century writing about the medieval period, the link between medieval peoples and modern concepts of race becomes overt, no longer an undercurrent of thought but the very basis for proving superiority of the old (racially pure) over the new (racially corrupt) peoples in Western societies. The entire Middle Ages became a *lieu de mémoire*, a historic touchstone that had to be continually revisited in the discourse of race.

Next, in reviewing the troubled relationship between "race" and medieval studies, I look in chapter 2 at the major currents of racial theory and the role of the Middle Ages in the ways these histories have been passed down. Race theorists, like others who come in contact with our medieval past, must grapple with the ever-present, though contested, desire to place a dividing line between the modern and the ancient, seeing the modern period as plagued by racial troubles and the earlier periods as free from that particular concern. Through medieval depictions of humans or human-animal hybrids we can glean a sense of what hierarchies were put in place in the premodern period and which of these orderings correspond to our definitions of racial thinking.

The centrality of Christianity to the European Middle Ages is without question, and chapter 3 turns to the various treatments of black skin in religious contexts. The Bible has few mentions of skin color, but as textual commentators focused on those passages, their cultural importance grew out of proportion to their number. Noah's sons became the ancestors of mankind following the Flood, and Moses married an Ethiopian. How did medieval commentators read these moments in biblical history in relation to the world and peoples around them? The queen of Sheba, an iconic black figure in the medieval imagination, represented different things for at least two medieval authors: Christine de Pizan and Boccaccio. Within that matrix of race and gender, anxieties of reproduction and lineage emerged that would find further root in secular literature.

Chapter 4 delves into medieval views on reproduction, inheritance, and miscegenation. Early scientific treatises on conception and on what would come to be called genetics show that medieval people did not necessarily see race as fixed or as something that could be passed along from parent to child. Because of our limited data set on medieval thought and practices, some questions will likely never be answered. Which of the medieval philosophies on difference was widespread enough to have clearly been passed on to later generations? Where did these ideas come from in the cultural context of medieval Christianity? Even without the answers to these clearly important questions, we begin to see some trends developing as early as the twelfth and thirteenth centuries. Religious conversion could literally change physical forms. On the other hand, doubts about conversion also left these forms mutable, to the point where bodies were destabilized, ever in danger of flipping back to other races, as it were. Medieval literature gives us both the attraction, the desire, for the racial Other and also the danger that the Other poses.

The medieval literature of fantastic encounter and possession of the Other laid the groundwork for colonial expansion, the subject of chapter 5. Fifteenth- and sixteenth-century explorers literally carried with them elements of medieval ideas about difference—as in the copy of Mandeville's *Travels* carried by Christopher Columbus. The mapping of older, medieval ideas onto and into new places shows the desire to relate what has come before to what one is currently experiencing. When Old World ideas were applied to New World peoples, they formed a basis for the racism endemic in Western societies in the modern period. As explorers found new routes and lands, they inevitably encountered new peoples, and the lands that had been uncharted, where they had placed fantastic peoples and dragons on early maps, now had names and real peoples. When these explorers traveled, they took their medieval travel accounts (even fictitious ones) with them as guidebooks, and they saw what they expected to see. Medieval ways of describing other races became modern ways of describing indigenous New World peoples, and medieval arguments about humanness were employed to justify the slave trade.

In lieu of a formal conclusion, in chapter 6 I explore some ways that the continuity between medieval and modern concepts of race plays itself out in twentieth- and twenty-first-century cultural production, pointing out how the medieval continues to play a role in our racial imagination, underlining the amount of work that remains to be done in our understanding of how the Middle Ages has been used and continues to be used in discourses of racism.

1

Remaking the Middle Ages

The nineteenth century was a key moment in the formation of what is now called medieval studies. While Renaissance writers and thinkers were concerned with separating themselves from a past that they saw as misguided and ignoble, by the nineteenth century the tide had turned, and the Middle Ages were not only established as a valid field of study but also entered popular culture as a time of great interest. Citing among their many and varied examples the holidays created to honor Joan of Arc and an outpouring of medieval novels, Elizabeth Emery and Laura Morowitz remark, "At the end of the nineteenth century, people from all over the political and social spectrum praised the Middle Ages and avidly consumed 'medieval' products."[1]

Currents of nationalism ran deep in the late nineteenth century, and much of the work of reconstructing the Middle Ages was put to the service of this ever-increasing need to distinguish and justify the histories of European geopolitical entities.[2] At the same time, the development of nineteenth-century European and American nationalism was intimately entwined with notions of race and scientific racism—the attempt to scientifically classify the differences between physical, mental, and even spiritual capacities of the varieties of mankind. Steeped in the important questions of nineteenth-century nationalism and racism, medieval scholars wrote histories, edited and published medieval texts, restored buildings, and codified exactly what we mean today by "medieval."

Scholars have begun the important work of uncovering the impact of nineteenth-century nationalism on the formation of medieval studies, but far less work has been done on the role of scientific racism on our memory of the medieval period. In order to come close to understanding medieval notions of racial difference, we need to remove, or at least question, the nineteenth-century perspective that was so formative in the creation of medieval studies. In short, we need to take off the nineteenth-century glasses through which we read the medieval era. The best way to do that is to first turn our perspective away from the medieval period and toward the nineteenth-century lens through which we are looking, so that we can understand the impact this period had on our own notion of what constitutes the Middle Ages. Let us begin with a nineteenth-century American writer and his vision of the medieval past.

Spanish History and Washington Irving's Notion of Degeneration

Even today in Granada, Spain, every souvenir store, corner newspaper stand, and even the shop at the Alhambra itself carries multiple translations of Washington Irving's 1832 *The Alhambra*. Most Americans know Irving from his early "Legend of Sleepy Hollow" and are likely unaware of this book described by Easton Press, a publisher of high-quality leather-bound books for collectors, as one of the "100 Greatest Books Ever Written." In reading *The Alhambra* it is clear why the book is translated and sold to tourists from around the world who visit Granada. As Ángel Flores notes in the introduction to the 1969 edition of Irving's work, Irving infuses his stories about medieval Spain with his own personality and the social preoccupations of early nineteenth-century America.[3] Flores finds echoes of American class struggle, women's liberation, and abolitionist discourse in the stories of conflicts between rebellious children and repressive parents.

In addition to the book on the Alhambra, however, a large portion of Washington Irving's oeuvre was dedicated to medieval Spain, and these works are for the most part overlooked by Irving scholars, who tend to be Americanists interested in his corpus centered on the American continent. Most recent work on Irving has highlighted his relationship with budding American national identity.[4] Yet it would be a mistake to see him simply as an "American" writer, for he was a well-read cosmopolitan writer with considerable social and intellectual influence in Europe as well as America. His familiarity with the ideas on race that circulated first in Europe and later in the United States is reflected in his fascination with miscegenation in *The Alhambra* and other writings on medieval Spain.

These attitudes in turn shaped and continue to shape American views of medieval Spain, and arguably even modern Spain.

Though born in New York, Irving moved to Europe for almost two decades at the height of his writing career. Just two years after arriving in England, he had made enough of a name for himself in literary circles to be invited to a dinner at the country's premier publishing house, Murray, which later published the first complete edition of his *Sketch Book*.[5] The *Sketch Book* was soon translated into German and French, and Irving became an internationally recognized author who frequented literary circles in England, France, Germany, and Spain. By the time he published *The Alhambra* at the age of nearly fifty, he had spent seventeen years in Europe, working in London, traveling and living in France and Germany, and serving in the U.S. diplomatic corps in Spain. Irving had evolved from a writer of quintessentially "American" tales to an international man of letters whose writings commented on the burning issues of nationalism and scientific racism of nineteenth-century Europe. In Europe, Irving found an intellectual milieu that was attempting to apply scientific principles to social questions, and he in turn recounted the medieval history of Spain in prose permeated with descriptions of racially linked degeneration more appropriate to his own American culture than to medieval Spain.

Irving's work was shaped by the obsession with ethnic purity and search for national origins that formed part of the intellectual climate of the early to mid-nineteenth century. That obsession was based on the work of University of Göttingen professor Johann Friedrich Blumenbach. A medical doctor, Blumenbach in 1775 wrote his M.D. thesis, *De Generis Humani Varietate Nativa* (*On the Natural Varieties of Mankind*), a treatise that is generally credited with the first use of "race" in the modern understanding of the word, as well as the term "Caucasian." In his treatise Blumenbach sets forth the idea that mankind originated in the Caucasus Mountains. From this privileged place of origin, man spread throughout the Earth, eventually forming the five races that existed in Blumenbach's worldview. The races, Caucasian, Mongolian, Ethiopian, Malay, and Amerindian, were ranked according to beauty, with the most attractive being the white Caucasian and the least attractive being the Mongolian and Ethiopian:

> I have allotted the first place to the Caucasian . . . which makes me esteem it the primeval one. This diverges in both directions into two, most remote and very different from each other; on the one side,

namely, into the Ethiopian, and on the other into the Mongolian. The remaining two occupy the intermediate positions between that primeval one and these two extreme varieties; that is, the American between the Caucasian and Mongolian; the Malay between the same Caucasian and Ethiopian.[6]

In Blumenbach's view the Semitic peoples, Arabs and Jews, form a part of the Caucasian race and thus can claim the superior beauty of the white race. Later thinkers would revise Blumenbach's thesis and see the Semitic as separate from the Caucasian,[7] but until the early twentieth century Semitic peoples were still seen as particularly imbued with certain facilities in the arts and certainly above the black, or Ethiopian, race.[8]

Blumenbach's work was immediately acclaimed and influential. Despite his insistence that mankind derived from a single race, his ideas would be transformed in the mid-nineteenth century in support of the supremacy of the Aryan race that supposedly first descended from the Caucasus.[9] Blumenbach had laid the groundwork for a separation of mankind. Rather than seeing the continuity and similarity between men everywhere, the divisions became a focus of interest and codified. These differences had been noticed before, of course, and travelers had reported encounters with odd, marvelous, or barbaric persons since the very first travel accounts. But once linked in the nineteenth century with a post-Darwinian notion of evolution and adaptation, these differences between peoples could be interpreted in a judgmental way—some people, or "races," were seen to have evolved or adapted in superior ways. Tracing one's lineage back to these originary forefathers indicated certain innate qualities or advantages, so the thinking went, that were passed along.

This genealogical method of thinking bled into other areas of analysis. Because the excellence of the present was "scientifically proven" to be indebted to the extraordinary ancestors in the past, a search for origins became an obsession. In literary studies this translated into a search for the earliest vernacular texts, like the epic *Chanson de Roland* in France.[10] These early texts needed characters to embody a certain spirit that would characterize the present nation. For *Roland*, the desirable traits might be bravery and loyalty. These qualities would be found in descendants of Frankish stock, although not necessarily in those who lived in France but had different ethnic or racial origins. One needed to search for one's roots to find the essence of one's own "stock."

Americans were not exempt from this genealogical obsession—far from it. The late nineteenth century saw the establishment of the Daughters of the American Revolution and Sons and Daughters of the Confederacy. For an American like Washington Irving, roots were sought not within America but within northern European lands. America was considered a "young" land, and the United States was a brand-new nation. Irving's turn toward Europe for the origins of America, and the popularity of his accounts of Europe and European history in the United States, illustrate the tremendous need to describe one's past in the intellectual climate of the early nineteenth century.

Inseparable from Irving's understanding of "origin" was the United States' preoccupation with slavery and its Native American population. While Europeans were writing their own histories and origins, many of them entwined with the ever-growing racist discourse of the period, Irving needed to account for the origins of the United States, a country whose foundation involved conquest and racial and social stratification despite overt claims of liberty for all. While this also posed a dilemma for European Enlightenment thinkers,[11] for American writers the need was more pressing. They had to look beyond their own borders to different lands to find, not an ethnically pure "first" American, but acceptable forebears from a circumscribed set of European countries.

Anxieties about miscegenation were particularly acute in the land that constituted the American frontier. Irving's attitude toward miscegenation is startling, as he describes the possible mixing of various American Indian tribes in his 1836 *Astoria*, a history of John Jacob Astor's Pacific Fur Company:

> It is to be feared that a great part of [the Far West] will form a lawless interval between the abodes of civilized man, like the wastes of the ocean or the deserts of Arabia. . . . Here may spring up mongrel races, like new formations in geology, the amalgamation of the "debris" and "abrasions" of former races, civilized and savage.[12]

But America was not the only place where Irving imagined that races "civilized" and "savage" formed a motley group.

Irving's interest in the history of medieval Spain was not accidental, for in medieval Spain he saw a cautionary model for the United States. For Irving, Spain had two great originary civilizations: the Gothic nomadic people that moved to the area in the late antique period and then the Islamic invaders of the Conquest. Irving did not see the Muslim Conquest as an undesirable moment in Spanish history,[13] just as he did not see the European conquest of North America in a negative light. Spain, having once seen the glory of a "new" nation founded through conquest and conflict, had aged, become degenerate as it lost its racial purity, and lost the grandeur it once possessed. For Irving's transfer of civilization from Europe to the Americas to be complete, the European had to be cast as weakened and effete in comparison to the vigorous young American. Irving's histories of Granada and the Alhambra led logically to his history of Christopher Columbus—the downfall of one civilization prompted the birth of another.

Irving painted Spain as degenerate due to the racial makeup of its people. From the outset, miscegenation and its effects lurked beneath the half-history, half-fantasy nature of *The Alhambra*. As Irving wrote in the preface of his 1851 revised edition:

> It was my endeavor scrupulously to depict its half Spanish half Oriental character; its mixture of the heroic, the poetic, and the grotesque; to revive the traces of grace and beauty fast fading from its walls; to record the regal and chivalrous traditions concerning those who once trod its courts; and the whimsical and superstitious legends of the motley race now burrowing among its ruins.[14]

This idea of mixing the East and West recurred throughout the book, as for example when Irving typified the stories of buried treasures left behind by the Moors as indicative of "that mixture of the Arabic and the Gothic which seems to me to characterize every thing in Spain, and especially the southern provinces."[15]

Irving opened the 1832 edition with a dedication to his friend and traveling partner:

> You may remember that, in the course of the rambles we once took together about some of the old cities of Spain, particularly Toledo and Seville, we frequently remarked the mixture of the Saracenic with the Gothic, remaining from the time of the Moors, and were more than once struck with incidents and scenes in the streets, that brought to mind passages in the "Arabian Nights."[16]

The people themselves bear the mark of the mixture of Goth and Moor, as seen in the description of the muleteer, the "legitimate traverser of the land."[17] Irving cast the muleteer thus: "His low, but clean-limbed and sinewy form betokens strength; his complexion is dark and sunburnt; his eye resolute, but quiet in its expression, except when kindled by sudden emotion; his demeanor is frank, manly, and courteous,"[18] "frank" and "manly" being words that Irving used elsewhere to describe the Goth, whereas the Moor is governed by emotion, dark, and courteous.

The Moors also left a lasting imprint, as illustrated by the proclivity toward song that the muleteer exhibits: "This talent of singing and improvising is frequent in Spain, and is said to have been inherited from the Moors."[19] On a foray into Granada, Irving again found traces of another culture, this time originating from the Arab homeland:

> If they caught my eye as I loitered by, they almost invariably invited me to partake of their simple fare. This hospitable usage, inherited from their Moslem invaders, and originating in the tent of the Arab, is universal throughout the land, and observed by the poorest Spaniard.[20]

Irving summed up the lingering mark of the Arab on Spain: "Thus the country, the habits, the very looks of the people, have something of the Arabian character."[21] Singing and courtesy were not the only legacies of the Moor, Irving disclosed immediately in the next sentence: "the general insecurity of the country is evinced in the universal use of weapons."[22] The mixture of Goth and Moor has led to a far more sinister configuration.

For Irving, Muslim Spain provided an initial experiment where the qualities of one race lined up against the proclivities of another. As Irving portrayed it, a civilized, or Semitic, race fought with African Berbers for political control. The ruling class was comprised of pure Arabs whom Irving characterized repeatedly as white.[23] While we have no way of knowing if Irving knew of Blumenbach's work, it is quite likely, and Blumenbach's classification of Arabs as Semitic had already been translated by others into a cultural superiority over black races.[24] This racial and class difference echoes the one that Irving projected onto medieval Spain:

> A grand line of distinction existed among the Moslems of Spain, between those of Oriental origin and those from Western Africa. Among the former the Arabs considered themselves the purest race, as being descended from the countrymen of the Prophet, who first raised the standard of Islam; among the latter, the most warlike and

powerful were the Berber tribes from Mount Atlas and the deserts of Sahara, commonly known as Moors, who subdued the tribes of the sea-coast, founded the city of Morocco, and for a long time disputed with the oriental races the control of Moslem Spain.[25]

In the 1851 edition of *The Alhambra*, illustrated by F.O.C. Darley,[26] "The Legend of the Arabian Astrologer" contains an illustration of the two types of Muslim implied in Irving's work—the white, pure Arab type astride his warhorse, and the duplicitous black Moor magician (fig. 1.1).[27] In this story, the Gothic princess manages to disdainfully avoid sexual relations with both of these men who are enamored of her.[28] She allows them to pamper her and give her riches, but as soon as they show interest in lovemaking, she plays her magical silver lyre, which puts them to sleep.

While the Gothic princess avoids miscegenation, Irving notes that, unfortunately for the historical Granada, intermarriage did eventually take place, and he traces the downfall of Boabdil, the last of the Muslim monarchs of Granada, and the end of the Muslim presence in Spain, to the outcome of miscegenation. At this point in Irving's story, the miscegenation is Muslim-Christian. Boabdil's father, ruler Muley Abul Hassan, first married his cousin, a highborn Muslim princess whose first son was Boabdil. In his old age, however, Boabdil's father married a beautiful Christian captive, whose children were supported in their bid for the throne by a rival faction. Two main families were involved in the dispute. The purest of the Muslims, the Abencerrages,[29] supported the full-blooded Muslim, Boabdil. Boabdil's mixed-race siblings were supported by the Venegas, themselves the mixed-race descendants of a noble Christian captive who was raised as a Muslim and scaled political heights as the vizier for Boabdil's father. When the dust cleared, the pure Arabs had been driven from Spain and the Christian-heritage Muslims reintegrated into the Spanish nobility.[30]

Throughout *The Alhambra*, Irving makes miscegenation a central part of the history of Spain. On the one hand, miscegenation contributes what he considers positive qualities to the national character of the Spanish, for instance abilities in singing and dancing and generous hospitality. On the other hand, not only do negative qualities such as excessive pride and fickleness also enter the mix, but miscegenation leads to the eventual downfall of the Moorish kingdom and, one is led to pre-

Figure 1.1. F.O.C. Darley, *The Spell-Bound Gateway*, in Washington Irving, *The Alhambra* (1851 edition), 187.

sume, the general decay of Spanish culture as compared with the vibrant young American culture. The original distinction Irving makes between the elite of the Muslim army and its rank and file, a difference that he color-codes as white for the elite and black for the slave class, creates a privileged Arab class that is sometimes (but not always) deemed worthy of intermarriage with pure Gothic Christians, but which denies to the black Muslim the same dignity that the white Muslim enjoys.

As Granada fell to Christian hands, the best of the Muslims, epitomized by the Abencerrages, either died defending the pure-blooded line of Arabs or left Spain, leaving their legacy imprinted in the land, its architecture, and the mixed blood of the Spaniards. However, the black Moors also left their legacy and mixed blood behind, forming a caste system in Spain. Spain, writes Irving, became a land ruled by vigorous Christian counts who had noble Arab blood, descending down the social scale to the effete *viejos cristianos*, or old Christians, who kept themselves impoverished but pure of black Moorish blood, and finally at the bottom the vagrant, robber-like gypsy descendants of the black Moors. In the architecture of the Alhambra and above all in the legends that residence in the Alhambra inspires him to reform, recast, and recount, Irving finds the lost glory of the elite Arabs, a pure Semitic people that can live again only through the art of the storyteller.

As one of America's first medievalists, Irving participated in the formation of an American medieval studies field that from its inception was deeply concerned with race. Irving's vision of the Middle Ages would not qualify as history in classes today, but it did in the nineteenth century, and it continues to be read and marketed as such in and around the Alhambra and by tourist organizations in Spain that use his work to promote a romantic view of Spain's Moorish past.[31]

The Alhambra put forth a vision of Spain that continues today in works that view medieval Spain as participating uniquely in a golden age of cohabitation and *convivencia*. Irving saw the mixture of Gothic and Moor as leading to the eventual downfall of the Spanish people. While invigorating Old Christian white blood with noble Semitic Muslim blood created an upper crust, the Gothic princess was correct to keep her bloodline pure because the danger of mixed blood was all too evident in the Spaniard of Irving's time. The notion of *convivencia*, or a time unique to the past when cultures lived side by side, is much like what Irving imagines this ideal past to have been. As long as each culture can keep separate and learn from the other, Irving is content with cultural contact. For him, assimilation, in the form of intermarriage, begins the inevitable downfall of great civilizations. Medievalists might learn from the negative example Irving gives us. By extension, this same critique might be made of *convivencia*, in that assimilation of any of the cultures would be seen as the end of the cohabitation or golden period. This idealization of a golden age in the past rarely accounts for the complexities of cultural contact and dynamism, instead reifying a mythical moment of cultural purity and discouraging cultural adaptation. Feelings of nationalism and ethnocentrism become inseparable from this mythical historical past.

Viollet-le-Duc's Architectural Bodies

In nineteenth-century Europe, reimagining the Middle Ages was a key component of rising sentiments of nationalism. All areas of what we now term the humanities were touched by the search for origins and the new-found interest in the Middle Ages as the very center of what it meant to be, say, French or German or Italian. Science was assigned the task of providing a rational basis for perceived differences between nationalities. This period saw the establishment of medieval studies as a discipline in European universities.[32] Outside the academy, governments employed academics and experts in the past to help write or even (re)construct the early histories of nations. As those stories were written, sometimes literally carved in stone in the case of the reconstruction of medieval cathedrals, nineteenth-century conceptions of the past became the stuff of the everyday world around us.

Perhaps no figure had greater impact on the reimagining of the Middle Ages than Eugène-Emmanuel Viollet-le-Duc, who was responsible for the restoration of French medieval architecture from about 1838 to 1879. He personally directed the restorations of Vézelay, where the First Crusade was born; Saint-Denis, the official seat of medieval French secular and ecclesiastical power; Notre-Dame de Paris, the best-known of all European medieval monuments; and many others. Responsible for restoring some of the most important sites of the Middle Ages, Viollet-le-Duc molded the perception of the European Middle Ages experienced by his own and subsequent generations, leading twentieth-century critic Max-Pol Fouchet to declare that "Vézelay is memory."[33] By his own admission, Viollet-le-Duc did not seek to restore the medieval artifacts to their state at some fixed time in the past, but he reworked the objects of his architectural endeavor to mold them to an ideal that, he determined through years of study and research, was what the state of the building should have been but most likely never was: "To restore a building is not just to preserve it, to repair it, and to remodel it, it is to re-instate it in a complete state such as it may never have been at any given moment."[34] Intellectuals of Viollet-le-Duc's time were deeply concerned with new ideas on technology and science, including debates surrounding the origins of the races, a dialogue that incorporated the results of Charles Darwin's 1831–36 voyage on the *Beagle* and the publication of his 1859 *On the Origin of Species*. Throughout this period, Europeans were literally obsessed with classifying and naming all aspects of the physical world, and in no arena more so than that of mankind itself. In this tumultuous period, the importance of man's origin and evolution held center stage, and almost every aspect of intellectual life dealt directly or obliquely with this issue. Even architectural theory, a field not apparently immersed in the biological basis of human development, saw the application of these ideas to its discipline.

Central to understanding the relationship between racial consciousness and architecture is the figure of Georges Cuvier (1769–1832), one of the most influential scientific researchers of the nineteenth century, who frequented the salon of Viollet-le-Duc's uncle, painter and critic Étienne-Jean Delécluze. Cuvier worked largely on fossils and the geological origins of the Earth, though his contributions extended into other areas of natural science as well. Though his refusal to accept evolution caused some of his theories to later fall into disrepute, his work was influential in the period immediately prior to the discoveries of Darwin and Lamarck. Among the most controversial aspects of his legacy is his work with the South African Khoi woman Saartjie or Sara Baartman, whom Europeans called the Hottentot Venus.

At the forefront of architectural theory,[35] Viollet-le-Duc greatly influenced not only architects of his own time but also those who followed.[36] Viollet-le-Duc lectured at the École des Beaux-Arts in Paris between November 1863 and March 1864. Although he had a tumultuous history with the École (Viollet-le-Duc repeatedly criticized the state of teaching the arts in nineteenth-century Europe) and was never accepted by the Beaux-Arts students or faculty, his lectures were recorded by Émile Alglave and appeared in the *Revue des cours littéraires de la France et de l'étranger* in 1864.[37] In these lectures he outlined his theory of architecture, which included a racially based explanation for the development of the arts, a theory he would later publish in greater detail.

One of Viollet-le-Duc's main preoccupations was with the aesthetics particular to a given people at a given time, based largely on his observations of architecture. This interest culminated in his 1875 *Histoire de l'habitation humaine* (*The Habitations of Man in All Ages*), which set forth the view that each race of people has an architectural style that is inherently proper to it based on the availability of local materials and the aesthetic possibilities proper to that race. This book's two protagonists, Epergos and Doxius, travel through time and space to witness the development of housing in mankind's history. With their Greek names, Doxius and Epergos serve the literal role of *translatio studii*,[38] as they pass on their knowledge of architecture and justice to the different groups they meet.

In the opening chapter, "Sont-ils des hommes?" [Are they men?], Doxius and Epergos meet a group of early men who have not yet discovered housing. Feeling pity for them, Epergos shows them how to bend young trees and make a rudimentary shelter (fig. 1.2). Doxius prefers a more hands-off approach, allowing mankind's housing to develop on its own. He challenges his friend, asking him if he would show a bird how to make a nest or a beaver a dam.[39] Epergos responds that, after all, "ces êtres ne sont pas des animaux" [these creatures are not mere animals], to which Doxius replies, "Folie! que seraient-ils donc alors?" [Folly! . . . what then can they be?].[40] Epergos defers the arguments, saying that he will check back in 100,000 days to see if what he has taught these prehumans has adhered or not.

The next chapter, presumably 100,000 days later, finds Epergos and Doxius face to face with Arya, a man who looks like the two companions and is the head of a large family.[41] According to Arya, his family has always lived in these mountains. At this point we find that Epergos and Doxius have not traveled through time but are instead in a different place (fig. 1.3) than when they showed the prehumans how to construct a shelter. Epergos tells Arya that up to this point they have encountered only "beings inferior to thee, living like the brutes on raw flesh and wild herbs,—not knowing how to build places of shelter,—naked and filthy."[42] Arya knows the beings and calls them the Dasyus, a cursed race that Indra will chase from the land that they sully and that rightfully belongs to the Aryas.

The two friends move through time and space until they reach the feu-

Figure 1.2. Epergos and Doxius travel back in time and encounter primitive people called the Dasyus. Epergos shows them how to build a basic dwelling. Eugène-Emmanuel Viollet-le-Duc, *Histoire de l'habitation humaine*, 6.

Figure 1.3. The Aryas, living at the same time, already possess architectural skills far more advanced than the Dasyus'. Eugène-Emmanuel Viollet-le-Duc, *Histoire de l'habitation humaine*, 11.

dal era, as Viollet-le-Duc terms it. Clearly influenced by medieval literary texts, Viollet-le-Duc has the two go on a pilgrimage that has all the elements of a chivalric *aventure*. In fact, when they are attacked feloniously by a nameless knight (in a plotline similar to Chrétien's *Yvain*), Viollet-le-Duc even uses the epic formula describing one of the blows as one that "would infallibly have cloven [the] skull to the very teeth."[43] While Viollet-le-Duc tells a gothic tale of treachery and revenge, the two Greek messengers explore the castle, relating the high points of the architecture of the feudal fortress. They also give the count who owns the fortress a message from his cousin who has been defending the Christian Holy Land against the Saracens. In this message, the cousin tells how to reinforce the fortress and upgrade fighting skills with technologies such as Greek fire.

For the two Greeks, civilization becomes a constant circle of birth, growth, and decay. As each civilization reaches its height and gives to the world its aesthetic contributions, that same society begins its downward descent because of decay and contamination. Only on the upward side of the cycle is each civilization true to its own origins and thus uses in a positive manner ideas and contacts with other civilizations. For Viollet-le-Duc, after the transmission of ideas from "Saracen" civilization, the European feudal order continues to develop an authentic, positive culture until the Renaissance. At that point the influx of foreign ideals, namely the renewal of ancient Greek and Roman architectural influences, results in an imbalance that sends the cycle downward.

Cultural borrowing is fine—to a point. After that point, a society loses touch with its origins and begins to mimic aesthetics that are inappropriate for its race and culture. Epergos takes the French Renaissance architect to task for his imitation of Greek and Roman forms, saying:

> Why then not remain simply what you are—... following your natural genius ... ? Why this somewhat childish return to forms which are quite out of harmony with your requirements and habits? ... You invented in France, more than three hundred years ago, a system of vaulting superior to that of the Romans ... [which] now you are abandoning. ... Why ... ? What good purpose can it serve?[44]

For Viollet-le-Duc, this fear of contamination or over-assimilation of foreign ideas shows up elsewhere. In examining the mixture of architectural elements in the Yucatán, he writes:

Whence we may conclude that the nation by which those buildings were constructed sprang from very diverse origins, or that they were a degenerate issue, subjected to influences from powerful races that had long cultivated the arts, but which had only imperfectly and rudely assimilated those influences,—had badly digested them, so to speak—and were, in especial, incapable of co-ordinating them, and choosing such elements as should be adapted to the climate and conditions in which circumstances had placed them."[45]

His ultimate goal is to reveal a sense of authentic race consciousness, a project that he does not seem to understand is doomed to failure because of the cultural contact and assimilation that he documents throughout *The Habitations of Man*. The culmination of architectural aesthetics will come about only when man understands his past and seeks architectural methods that are appropriate to that past. He describes the mission as follows:

In regard to human habitations the result of the inquiry will be that each will become acquainted with the elementary characteristics of his race or of the races from which he is descended; and such knowledge will enable him to improve his dwelling in accordance with his natural proclivities and aptitudes.[46]

Acknowledging influence by Arthur de Gobineau's 1851 *Essai sur l'inégalité des races humaines* (*The Inequality of Human Races*), Viollet-le-Duc finds that those descended from the Aryas will achieve the closest to aesthetic perfection through their contact with the Semite peoples. Those descended from the Dasyus, the accursed race that he deems prehuman, are incapable of the same artistic and aesthetic accomplishments. That these Dasyus are later to be found in black Africa is made clear in his 1864 course "Esthétique appliquée à l'histoire de l'art" at the École des Beaux-Arts, where he writes:

Let us first establish certain general facts that dominate these questions [of aesthetics]. The human races are not equal and, to speak only of the two extremes, it is obvious that the white races that have covered Europe for three thousand years are infinitely superior to the Negro races that have lived since time immemorial in a large part of Africa. The first have a regular history, a succession of civilizations more or less perfected, moments of surprising splendor; the others are today where they were twenty centuries ago, and their contact with the civilization of European peoples has had no other result than to teach them needs and vices of which they were unaware without making them enter into the path of true progress.[47]

According to this version of aesthetic history, only when the Aryan imbued with strength and command learns aesthetic appreciation through contact with the East can a society reach the pinnacle of aesthetic achievement.

What might this mean for the medievalist hoping to understand difference and cultural contact in the Middle Ages? Historians of art like Viollet-le-Duc who have such a profound impact on our cultural memory have the ability to shape our views of the past in ways both evident and hidden. When we examine the conceptions of Notre-Dame de Paris, Pierrefonds, Vézelay, and the like, do we see medieval architecture or do we see the application of nineteenth-century scientific racism to what passes as our collective memory of the Middle Ages? Since Viollet-le-Duc boldly proclaimed that he set out to remake the Middle Ages as the period that never was but should have been, to what extent can we trust the Middle Ages that we have made and remade since 1850?

A critical view of the Middle Ages and of medieval artifacts including art and literature must acknowledge the possibility that nineteenth-century fashionings of the Middle Ages have shaped our perception of medieval societies in ways that are extremely difficult to see but that are nonetheless profound. As we examine the question of medieval views on race, we cannot make blanket assumptions either about medieval notions of race or about their relevance to our period. As we attempt to study the past, we need to peel away the layers of interpretation that cover both the past and its artifacts. There will doubtless be moments of opacity where we cannot reliably reconstruct medieval attitudes toward the Other and must admit a certain amount of defeat in our understanding of the past. This, however, is a more honest approach than one that presupposes either a complete rupture with the past or blindness to historicity. Let us return now, like Epergos and Doxius, to the medieval period.

2

Medieval Race?

The decision to include the European Middle Ages in a history of race studies is far from obvious, particularly when the definition of race is fundamentally based on skin color.[1] The modern period, roughly from 1700 to the present, has had a privileged position vis-à-vis race studies, and for good reason. However, ideas concerning the origins, types, and worth of mankind did not spring up suddenly in the eighteenth century. Rather, these questions had been debated for centuries by European intellectuals and had found expression in the art and literature of periods far earlier than 1700.

In considering the history of race, one of the first things to establish is the distinction between race and racism and to treat the history of these two concepts separately. "Race" and "racism" are two different terms, with one definition of "race" being a group that shares some socially selected *physical* traits, as opposed to "ethnicity," which is defined by socially selected *cultural* traits.[2] Racism, as opposed to race, places a valuation on these physical traits and ranks humans according to them, allowing for those with supposedly greater capacities to wield power over those with innately lower capacities.[3]

Twentieth-century historians of race looked to the eighteenth and nineteenth centuries, periods that brought discussions about and justifications of slavery in America. Eighteenth- and nineteenth-century debates concerning who should be considered a citizen, who should be allowed to vote, whether people could be considered property, and the like were central to the very idea of what the fledgling democracy stood for. The importation of black Africans across the Atlantic to the

New World marked a turning point in the history of the idea of race. Allowing slavery to continue in a country founded on the idea of equality required justifying this behavior by discounting the humanity of black Africans. Such a decision led inexorably to the institutionalization of the belief that some people are worth more than others—and, to take it a step further, that some people are not even human—based upon their appearance and origins. A similar line of thinking in Europe set the stage for the genocides of the twentieth century.

Histories of racism sometimes start in the sixteenth century, with a cursory note that the Spanish at this time articulated an idea of the "purity of blood," giving different rights and privileges based on how far back one could trace one's genealogy to Christian, rather than Jewish or Muslim, origins.[4] For others seeking the history of racial ideas, the origin of the word "race" is extremely important. Charles de Miramon finds the earliest uses of the word in fifteenth-century French poetry, where *race* refers to the bloodlines of certain dogs that stand as metaphors for French nobility. This connection with class, Miramon concludes, indicates that "race and hereditary blood were not initially racist. . . . The dominant medieval discourse leaves little room for a concept of race or human sub-species."[5] Pierre H. Boulle links the word "race" from the outset to the animal world, from the Italian usage in horse breeding.[6] For Boulle, the concept of class first became intertwined with the origins of the modern notion of race in the seventeenth century, epitomized in the dark-skinned peasants of La Bruyère.[7]

Both de Miramon and Boulle point to important changes in the way that the word "race" evolved in meaning in France over time. However, their philological insistence misses the point that meaning is also produced outside etymology. Though earlier writers were not using the particular word "race," they were dealing with shared socially selected physical traits, which we earlier defined as race. It is not necessary to have the word "race" to have the concept of race. So when John Mandeville describes the pygmies as being short, he is making a racial comment. Were he to imply somehow that being taller made another group of people superior to the pygmies, that would be a racist remark.[8]

Objecting that the word "race" does not have the same meaning for us today as it could possibly have had in the medieval context is quite correct. As has been pointed out, race has little or no biological meaning, and it can mean different things to different members of the same family, let alone to people separated by millennia and continents. Indeed, notions of difference in the Middle Ages were very different from those in twenty-first-century American society. Likewise, however, there are vast differences between what the word "race" means in our own day in France, Germany, Spain, the United States, and even from community to community and individual to individual within any one of these countries.[9] A search for an unchanging, stable connotation for the word "race" (or almost any word) across time and space would be unlikely to meet with success. Applying the word "race" to a different time and space tends to imply that there is in fact a constant notion of race, when today the thought that there is a significant biological difference between peoples and that everyone could be placed in a neat category seems hopelessly outmoded. All the same, the word does mean something today and has meant something in the past.[10] Coining a new word to apply to the medieval period (suggestions have included "chromotism," which would indicate that medieval peoples did find white superior to black, but that this did not constitute what we call racism)[11] seems designed to force the medieval period into an uncomfortable dichotomy with the modern period. With denial that the medieval period was haunted by preoccupations about difference, the Middle Ages emerges as either a golden age of cohabitation or a time of hopeless infancy, where peoples may have held notions of prejudice but were unable to articulate them.[12]

Not all race theorists see the premodern period through such rose-colored glasses. As early as 1983, Christian Delacampagne suggested that racism had its roots in the ancient and medieval West.[13] Colbert Nepaulsingh opines that racism is found throughout the world, not just among white Europeans, and that "This universal characteristic of racism is true not only for this century but for as long as we have recorded history."[14] He discusses the origin of the T-O map based on the sons of Noah and the "curse of Ham" to illustrate his point that the notion of racial difference did indeed exist in the Middle Ages. In a contemporaneous article, the same T-O map is analyzed by Suzanne Conklin Akbari, who carefully charts the ambiguous history of these early maps of the world that divided a flat, round earth into three unequal parts separated by major riverlike bodies of water.[15] The three parts of the world were usually attributed to Europe, Asia, and Africa, or even Ham, Shem, and Japheth, the sons of Noah who served as the founders of mankind's originary "races" in Christian racial discourse. Akbari shows that these maps were inconsistently labeled and that it would be centuries before a stable iconography emerged and even longer before cartographers thought of the world in binaries such as Occident and Orient.[16] Akbari thus nuances Nepaulsingh's location of premodern race consciousness, pointing to the importance of a dialogue between race theorists and medievalists—not that these two groups need to be mutually exclusive.

Additional recent work, however, has begun to uncover the extent to which color prejudice and antiblack sentiment was woven into the fabric of premodern culture.[17] Early on in Christian culture—borrowing from ancient cultures—the color black was associated with death and the underworld. Church fathers Paul and Origen extended the metaphor, equating black with sin, and Origen associated the darkness of sin with that of the "Ethiopian."[18] From that point, devils and demons were also conflated with black and with black people, or Ethiopians.[19]

Kofi Omoniyi Sylvanus Campbell finds colonial desire expressed as early as 1245 in Bartholomaeus Anglicus's *De proprietatibus rerum*, located in the Englishman's gaze upon the African landscape and inhabitants. By describing the Ethiopians in primitivizing terms, Bartholomew sets the stage for a colonial empire that will make use of the marvelous resources that the Ethiopians are not culturally advanced enough to use for themselves.[20] As Campbell's fascinating analysis shows, the precolonial discourse of medieval English literature is essential to the history of the Anglophone black Atlantic. Only by portraying black Africans as both culturally inferior and in need of containment can the colonial enterprise take hold.

So if we wish to look at the long history of race—more specifically, race as defined by the socially selected physical trait of skin color—and color prejudice in the West, what then is the role of the Middle Ages in that history? Did black skin correlate with moral qualities?

The medieval period lacks a univocal discourse of race. Dark skin does not always indicate the same thing, in that some dark-skinned people have admirable qualities, such as the black Saint Maurice.[21] In some cases, dark skin is closely linked to class, as historian Paul Freedman points out.[22] In the twelfth-century French tale of Aucassin and Nicolette, dark skin is related to both race and class, where a dark peasant complains of his lot and Nicolette wears blackface to pass herself off as a Muslim minstrel. Geraldine Heng recounts the obsession of Peter Abelard with black-skinned women, good for "private pleasure,"[23] and concludes that dark skin color did not always imply a total rejection. Even this seemingly more positive view of the black female body raises many troublesome issues—the women are better kept in private and not paraded about, perhaps from embarrassment or fear of angry outbursts; the skin is appreciated only for the effect it has on the masculine pleasure. Tellingly, black skin could acquire meaning only in contrast to the implied norm, white skin. However, it would be a fallacy to find a few positive examples of black-skinned people and conclude that the period was "race blind."[24] Excessive praise of black skin may only serve to point out the exceptionality of the person described: context is key.

In the same manner as the medieval English depictions of black Africa and Africans that Campbell writes about, other aspects of medieval discourse on the Other were formative in the Western discourse on race and essential to the burgeoning rhetoric of colonization and repression. One of these central questions is what constitutes a human being. Colin Dayan, writing on the institution of slavery in the Caribbean, points out that the person/thing dichotomy is essential to the establishment of slavery:

> the very incommensurability of persons and things was necessary to underpin the institution of slavery. . . . Examples ranging from proofs of animality to marks of reason or imbecility—and a great deal in between—became part and parcel of judicial work. The limits of personhood and the extension of thinglikeness became oddly inseparable in this landscape of coercion.[25]

As medieval writers categorized the beings that they encountered, some of the discussions on humanness reached levels that touch on premodern notions of race.

Medieval people tended to see certain markers for humanness that might today seem outrageous or quaint. Pygmies were ousted from the human category by some for not having enough "quantity" of humanness, while others declared them definitively human.[26] For medieval thinkers, the limit between man and beast was complicated.[27] Certainly, at times animals found themselves too closely aligned with the human, for instance the unfortunate pigs who at various places in fourteenth-century France were convicted and executed on murder charges—just a few of many animals treated on equal footing with humans in the legal process.[28] If animals could sometimes be treated as almost human, men could slip into nonhumanness. Adhering to the Christian religion, organizing in political groups such as kingdoms, and wearing clothing were all ways to demonstrate rational thought, and thus humanness.

On the other hand, people belonging to civilizations that lacked any one of these markers were open to accusations of nonhumanness.[29] In his encyclopedia, Bartholomaeus Anglicus lists those who do not get married (with apparently no other distinction) and those who do not wear clothing alongside beings without heads, troglodytes, and dog-people.[30] Medieval people long wondered whether these sorts of beings could be considered human and, if so, whether they had souls or not. Despite their bodily similarities with humans, cynocephali or dog-headed men were declared by Augustine to be nonhuman because they barked rather than talked, not because of their appearance.[31]

These basic questions about humanity versus nonhumanity, or "thing-likeness" as Dayan names it, were already being asked about people within some medieval communities. On a spiritual level, some Christian writers questioned whether everyone had a soul or not, creating a dual-layered categorization of people in which some were privileged by God from the outset. The twelfth-century canonist Gratian, for example, quotes Augustine, who denies claims that all human beings were created in the image of God by declaring in no uncertain terms that "mulier non est facta ad Dei imaginem" [woman is not made in the image of God].[32] The link between sexism and racism is not unlikely; as long as there was a hierarchy of souls for any reason, there was a tendency to refine and define relative positions in this chain.

In like manner, the French abbot Peter the Venerable (d. 1156) questioned the humanness of Jews. In one fictitious "dispute" between a Christian and a Jew, Peter presents a stalwart Christian who tries to convince a Jew of the superiority of Christianity to Judaism. Peter's polemic is harsh; since the Jews do not recognize the Truth, Peter says, they must be irrational. The Christian tells his Jewish interlocutor:

> I do not dare to call you a man, lest I be found lying greatly; for I recognize that reason—which separates man from the beasts and lifts him above them—is dead in you and buried. . . . Why should you not rather be called a brute animal, why not a beast, why not a horse?[33]

At this uncomfortable juncture between religions, the Jew is configured as an animal because of his lack of belief.

Medieval thinkers and writers were prepared to question the very humanness of the Other—whether dog-human hybrids, naked people from other cultures, women, or Jews—long before the first slave ships sailed for the Americas. Anti-Semitism and misogyny in particular played a crucial role in developing the rhetoric of thinglikeness on which the later colonial enterprise depended.[34]

It is therefore not surprising that postcolonial theorists have added much to the nuanced discourse on race that can be applied to medieval ideas about race as well as to the colonial period.[35] When cultures collide, as they did in the Crusades and during the colonial period, perceptions of self and Other are necessarily central. While the Crusades and the colonial period are very different eras, certain concepts developed by postcolonial theorists can be immensely useful in understanding the various ways medieval authors represented the Other.

For example, Homi Bhabha's discussion of mimicry illuminates the complex bind in which subjects are caught as they attempt to assimilate to the colonial culture but are never quite able to be accepted as full participants. He tells how the colonized subject of color can take on many aspects of the culture of the colonizer but not ever be fully "white," staying "almost the same but not white."[36] Bhabha's not-quite-assimilated colonized subject reminds the medievalist of the continued questions that surrounded Jews, Muslims, and pagans who converted in the Middle Ages. In both fictional and historical accounts, these converts are surround by a miasma of doubt about the efficacy or completeness of their conversions.

According to another postcolonial theoretical framework proposed by Bhabha and others, when colonizer and colonized live in the same physical place, a "third space" arises where elements of both cultures become the norm, a culture of hybridity.[37] This third space allows aspects of the cultures of both colonizer and colonized to mutate, collide, and take on new forms. While it is important to keep in mind the tragedy and even violent nature of this cultural cohabitation, the hybridized nature of the third space gives the colonized a certain amount of power to influence the culture of the colonizer. For the medievalist, this concept is not difficult to grasp, as so much of early European culture can be attributed to the influence of other cultures. The *convivencia* (a highly contested term that we will explore later), or living together of Christians, Jews, and Muslims in medieval Spain, was a third space that had enormous impact on the modern world.

Hybridity can also be seen within a single individual. In medieval Europe, one manifestation of this would be religious hybridity, referring not to those who seem to have converted wholly but to those who carried with them elements of their former religion to form a hybrid character. In terms of mimicry ("almost the same but not white") they are Christians, but not quite.[38] Medieval European literature is rife with these characters, some of whom convert presumably to enjoy certain benefits of the religion of their conquerors, like the Muslim giant Rainouart, part of the Guillaume d'Orange epic cycle, and the Muslim queen of Zazamanc in Wolfram von Eschenbach's *Parzival*.[39] In the queen of Zazamanc's case, her conversion fails to bring her the desired outcome—marriage to the icon of Germanic knighthood, Gahmuret. Christian, but not quite, she passes her hopes on to her mixed-race son, the black and white Feirefiz. He too is never fully assimilated.

The giant Rainouart is a tailor-made example of Bhabha's concept of mimicry. Just as he converts and is never quite right—his gigantic and dark physical appearance, his misunderstanding of Christian doctrine, his "chivalric" comportment—his attempts to do what his fellow Christian knights do provide a laugh. But this laugh is in fact directed not only at the "mimic man" Rainouart but also at the culture he is trying to mimic. His rejection by the monks in *Moniage Rainouart* illustrates the crafty and inhospitable nature of this set of Christian monks, just as his mistreatment at the hands of King Louis serves to show us how a Christian ruler is not supposed to act.

But while postcolonial theory can help us understand the medieval period, the medieval period describes and makes possible the very notions that postcolonial theory will eventually explore. Race theory helps us understand the Middle Ages, but race theory itself could not be developed without the long history that the premodern era offers. The relationships that formed during the colonial period between dominant and dominated are rooted in that long history of questioning the humanness of those who differ from a socially defined norm: physically, culturally, religiously, and so on. Étienne Balibar, in thinking about this relationship between those in control of power and those who are exploited, notes the importance of the subjugated in the formation of the dominant group's identity. He writes that "a dominant discourse is one that *reflects the contradiction with its 'other' within itself,* and makes this reflection the intrinsic motive of its own development."[40] In order to see how Balibar's dominant group constructs its own identity against that of those it dominates, we must understand how the dominant group has come to understand the dominated. It is not simply the moment when the dominant group gains the means to actually persecute the Other that constitutes the "moment" of race, but rather that moment is the culmination of interactions between two groups that have constructed their own identity in opposition to the ways that the other group is perceived. Balibar concludes, "In the end, we will get to the hypothesis that what makes a 'dominant ideology' is not a generalization of the values or opinions of the 'dominant,' but rather of the 'dominated,' subjects."[41]

I would suggest that medieval travel writing, ethnographies, and/or descriptions of other peoples enter into the dominant-dominated discourse with which Balibar is concerned. Even when no actual political domination is involved—though this is precisely what the Crusades sought[42]—the very act of writing and describing the Other is an attempt to dominate and control that other person (or culture or practice). This notion is a supplement to what Linda Lomperis suggests, which is that travel writings (ethnographies) "tend to produce the very 'others' that they also purport to describe,"[43] so that while travel writing may indeed produce a dominated subject, that dominated subject produces the dominant ideology. In Lomperis's view of travel writing, which would also hold for medieval travel writing, the traveler writes in order to understand, describe, and delineate the people, places, and things seen or heard about in the course of the voyage. The act of inscribing is also an act of circumscribing or containing that subject within the travel narrative. This does not imply an actual immediate domination of the subject of the narrative, but it is a figurative control that is placed on the subject of the travel narrative.

An example of this dynamic is found in the thirteenth-century *History of the Mongols*, a travel account written by the friar John of Plano Carpini during the course of his stint as Pope Innocent IV's ambassador to the court of the Great Khan. The account is remarkable for its description of the customs of the Mongols, including palace etiquette, and the tales of palace intrigue that took place during the Franciscan monk's sojourn there.

Lomperis describes Plano Carpini's account as "a mirror of his own subjective concerns,"[44] citing specifically his description of Mongol gender relations as revealing the monk's own preoccupation with conventional gender hierarchies. While it is the case that his description of gender roles for the Mongols tells us about the friar's own understanding of gender relations, it is also true that the Mongols in turn shaped Christian society. Plano Carpini's account was popular at the time, and elements of his report found a place in the enormously influential *Speculum historiale*, an encyclopedic work written and compiled by Vincent of Beauvais in the thirteenth century.[45]

As an example, Vincent had a heavy hand in editing and compiling, particularly the parts of Plano Carpini's narration having to do with marital relations.[46] Within an orderly account, Vincent draws in two narratives from other parts of Plano Carpini's travels, sandwiching a cautionary tale between entries about unusual Mongol marriage customs.[47] The tale is twofold: Mongols do not differentiate between legitimate and illegitimate sons, and Mongols supported an illegitimate son over a legitimate son for succession to the throne in Georgia. Between these unfamiliar marriage practices, easily seen in Western medieval Europe as immoral and perverted, Vincent implicitly warns the West about the need to define clear inheritance laws. Mongols, linked to sexual deviancy, do not have firstborn succession. Particularly in thirteenth-century France when succession rights were not clear—Louis IX was crowned at age twelve, with his mother as a regent to ward off potential rivals to the crown—linking primogeniture to morality and social order was an overtly political move on Vincent's part. Vincent's work in turn influenced European culture enormously, serving as a major reference up until the eighteenth century. Christian culture was constructed in opposition to other cultures, including Mongol culture. While Christians could not politically or physically dominate the Mongols, the act of describing Mongol society, criticizing it, and subordinating it (on vellum) to Christian civilization begins the cultural work necessary to produce the dominated subject; it is the same work that will be taken up during the colonial period to produce the racial subject.

D. Fairchild Ruggles's study of the importance of white-skinned "Christian" women in the social formation of the Hispano-Umayyad rulers of al-Andalus gives us an example of how a dominated culture might ultimately exert major influence on the culture of the dominator. These originally Christian mothers, slaves and concubines, provided a conduit for the mixing of Hispano-Umayyad and Christian cultures as well as genetic materials. In other words, the dominated slave women served to shape the dominant discourse of Muslim al-Andalus. Ruggles describes the gendering of race in al-Andalus, where the Umayyads intentionally had children not with their Muslim wives, but with Christian women, often described as fair and/or blond, in order to protect the succession from the claims that rival families of Hispano-Umayyad women could bring. Many of these children are also described as fair and blue-eyed. Because the Muslim culture traced lineage through the men, children of these white mothers were fully Muslim and able to inherit, but they stood outside the broader network of Hispano-Umayyad nobility.[48]

This use of genealogy (and eugenics *avant la lettre*) to produce the ideal heir finds its counterpart in the literature of Christian Europe. Christian rulers marry "Saracen" women in these literary tales, but these women too are fair and white. In an interesting turnabout, it would almost seem the Christian men are recapturing and marrying the Christian concubines (or their offspring) that the Muslims procured. This could explain in part the facility of conversion that we see among these women—they were always Christian, at least somewhere in the past, and they simply return to their roots. One example of this is the Count of Pontieu's daughter in the thirteenth-century French text named for her. Captured by a Muslim sultan, she converts and marries him, living a seemingly peaceful life until the sultan captures her French father and ex-husband. She saves their lives and escapes with them, converting back to Christianity and taking with her the son she bore the sultan. Switching back and forth between religions and cultures seems fairly simple for this woman.

The gendered picture of intermarriage and reproduction was necessarily different in the West because of Western laws concerning inheritance. Because inheritance at that time was not traced solely through the masculine line, Christian dynasties preferred that their offspring come from legitimate wives, who were by definition Christian, since interfaith marriages were officially prohibited. Women could inherit as well, as is illustrated by the well-known example of Eleanor of Aquitaine taking her lands with her to not one but two royal marriages. The somatic or bodily markers from a mixed marriage had very different meanings in Muslim and Christian cultures. Whiteness inherited from the mothers might be acceptable to Muslim rulers as a mark that there is no other claim on the throne; a similar somatic marker would indicate the exact opposite to

Christians. Dark skin could suggest an illegal union between Christian and Muslim, leaving a taint on the genealogical claim to inheritance.

Taint, the word coming into English from the Old French *teint*, is the stain, the marking that cannot be removed even after the washing of religious baptism. Whereas many race theorists have sought to differentiate premodern and modern race by relying upon religion, Lisa Lampert has noted how recent events and racial profiling have re-turned us toward a premodern notion of race, as articulated by Kwame Anthony Appiah.[49] Lampert points to Appiah's "Race" essay, where he finds that prior to the modern period religion was the primary indicator of difference and skin color was a marker of disbelief, not the cause of that disbelief.[50] For Lampert, post-9/11 profiling to locate Muslim extremists represents a return to Appiah's premodern notion of race, in which skin color indicates religion.[51]

The external appearances of medieval literary figures such as Rainouart and the king of Tars and Feirefiz were strong indicators of their origins and their irrevocable Otherness. A giant, a black king, and a black-and-white-striped knight stood out physically in ways that pointed directly to their dubious character. However much these men may have provided enjoyment to the medieval audience, that pleasure could never overcome the taint of difference. What happened when they converted to Christianity? If, indeed, their bodies were simply an indicator of their religion, did they change? Were their mutable bodies fully Christianized? Is the body simply an indicator of religion, or does the body itself continue to have an inherent defect that cannot be erased by a conversion?

Just as nineteenth-century scientists sought to prove that certain body types and brain configurations had related moral strengths and limitations, we could argue that the monstrosity inherent in the Other in the Middle Ages was not always mutable upon conversion, and even when transformed it almost never indicated a complete cleansing of moral values. Put another way, when the nineteenth-century physician Cesare Lombroso examined the skulls of hundreds of deceased criminals and wrote his influential study of how criminals could be identified by bumps on the head, he put a scientific stamp on the notion that the human body *is* the destiny of the person inside. A man could be "born criminal," and so identified by the shape of his skull.[52] A person with a criminal skull could not be trusted. Indeed, job interviews in the nineteenth century sometimes included trips to a phrenologist to determine the trustworthiness of the candidate. These nineteenth-century skull bumps were read and conclusions were reached about the impossibility of human goodness in ways strikingly similar to how the black body in medieval literature could indicate an inability for an individual to become fully "good."

ॐ

Why are the Middle Ages such a contested ground in the history of race? In his thought-provoking piece for a special issue of the *Journal of Medieval and Early Modern Studies* on race in the Middle Ages, William Chester Jordan suggests that the concept of race should not be pushed back to the Middle Ages, because race has no real scientific basis. In his example, a family with what census officials would term a black father and a white mother produces children who identify themselves in varying ways, not only culturally but also biologically.[53] If modern society's preoccupation with race and ethnicity has nuanced the field to the point that meaningful racial labels are difficult to produce, does this imply that the concept of race is no longer useful? For that reason, Jordan's question cuts to the heart of the theoretical conundrum faced by scholars of premodern race: what is the point of the inquiry? One purpose might be to question the radical break between the modern and premodern eras. The concept that everything suddenly changed in 1600 or 1700 or even 1800 (the date changes depending upon the period with which the scholar is most familiar) prevents serious inquiry into similarities and diachronic developments in mankind's history and is also often associated with a sense of the premodern as a dark, regressive period unrelated to the general march toward the betterment of mankind through technological progress.[54] By locating racial or even racist ideas in the very origins of the western Europe, it becomes clear that the scientific racism that developed from the seventeenth to the nineteenth century in Europe was not an unfortunate, chance development in the history of European civilization. Instead, the concept of racial difference began in the infancy of European civilization. Scientific racism was the inevitable outcome of the centuries of thought that preceded it. By understanding just how formative and ingrained the idea of race is in the European imagination, we could potentially not only avoid repeating the mistakes of the past but also better understand our own present.

In her trenchant and insightful argument for the study of race in the Middle Ages, Geraldine Heng states:

Thus fictionalized as a politically unintelligible time, because it lacks the signifying apparatus expressive of, and witnessing, modernity, medieval time is then absolved of the errors and atrocities of the modern, while its own errors and atrocities are shunted aside as essentially non-significative, without *modern* meaning, because occurring outside the conditions structuring intelligible discourse on, and participation in, modernity and its cultures. The replication of this template of temporality—one of the most durably stable replications in the West—is the basis for the replication of race theory's exclusions.[55]

In other words, the danger is real. If the medieval period is allowed to in essence "get away with" its part in the history of prejudice, whether classist or racist or sexist, because of its distance from today, then other times and places can also come to be seen as nonessential to the course of human history. The Western, the here, the now, the "modern" becomes exclusionary, self-contained, exclusively allowed to be worth studying and criticizing—a perilous view of the past if ever there was one.

3

Biblical Race

The centrality of religion to questions of difference in the Middle Ages seems obvious. Most conflict and encounter between Others in medieval literature touch on religion in one way or another: Christian warrior battles Saracen emir,[1] Saracen princess falls in love with Christian knight, Christian traveler meets pagan peoples. Skin color is often mentioned, but religion and skin color are not necessarily aligned.

What seems obvious—the alliance of religion and difference in the Middle Ages—turns out, however, to be more complicated than a first glance at works such as the *Song of Roland* might indicate. Looking at the treatment of blackness in the Bible, the central text of the Latin West, and subsequent reception and rewriting in the European Middle Ages provides a useful context for understanding how race evolved as a concept in the medieval West.

The Christian Bible says little about race. Romans, Egyptians, Babylonians, and Jews—all members of a common Mediterranean world—are distinguished primarily by their religious beliefs and cultural practices rather than their color. The few biblical episodes that do mention color were exploited to the fullest in both medieval commentaries on the texts and the medieval Christian imagination. Of the three biblical characters traditionally considered to be black, the first of these, Ham, features centrally in "origin of blackness" myths. The other two, the Queen of Sheba and Moses' Ethiopian wife, are essential to medieval discourse about miscegenation fears through their sexual connections to Jewish men. Perhaps not surprisingly, questions of gender become entangled with representations of color difference.[2]

The Ethiopian Bride

In Numbers 12:1, Moses, one of the pillars of Judeo-Christian religion, marries an Ethiopian woman, causing his brother and sister, Aaron and Miriam, to speak against Moses.[3] God—not Moses—responds to their complaints by cursing Miriam, appropriately or ironically turning Miriam's skin white with leprosy.[4]

A great deal of both ancient and modern ink has been spilled attempting to explain how this union either does not constitute interracial marriage or does not result in miscegenation. Some commentators claim that the Ethiopian woman was actually white.[5] Others claim that Moses never actually slept with her, so he and the lineage remained "pure." The Hellenistic Jewish historiographer Artapanus, believed to have lived in the third or second century BCE, catalogues Moses's time in Ethiopia but does not mention his marriage to an Ethiopian woman. In the first century CE, Romano-Jewish historian Flavius Josephus incorporates Artapanus's Ethiopian history into his own work but adds a story already familiar to ancient Greek writers: the betrayal of a besieged city by a royal daughter who falls in love with the leader of the attacking forces. In this case Tharbis, the daughter of the king of Ethiopia, watches Moses from the ramparts and falls in love with him due to his military prowess. She proposes marriage by way of a messenger, and he accepts, provided that she surrender the town. In Josephus's text, the nuptials are celebrated and Tharbis returns with Moses to Egypt.[6]

By about the tenth century, the love story has an important new twist. In the medieval Hebrew text *The Chronicles of Moses*, Moses stays in Ethiopia but never consummates his marriage with the Ethiopian woman:

> Moses captured the city and was placed upon the throne of the kingdom. . . . They also gave him the Cushite wife of the late Monarch. But Moses, fearing the God of his Fathers, did not approach her. . . .
>   In the fortieth year of his reign . . . the queen said to the princes: "Behold now, during the whole of the forty years . . . he has not once approached me."[7]

At least in this version, the Ethiopian woman is seen to be an unacceptable bride for Moses, and she herself announces that the marriage has never been consummated.

Debates about the identity—and more obsessively the race—of Moses's wife continue to this day. A basic online search for "Moses wife" will bring up a variety of long discussions about Zipporah or Moses's wife, and the meaning of "Ethiopian" and "Cushite," along with their historical derivations and potential usages. These modern commentaries echo the long ancient and medieval commentary tradition for the very brief mention of this marriage.

One of the most interesting modern interpretations of Moses's Ethiopian bride is the 2005 semihistorical biography by Marek Halter, a French-Jewish author living in Paris. The book, *Zipporah*, is part of a series on biblical women, which also includes *Lilah*, *Sarah*, and *Mary of Nazareth*.[8] The author made race the central aspect of Zipporah's life story, casting her as an adopted Cushite who is unmarriageable because she is black. Tellingly, the cover art for different editions reflects the continuing debate over Zipporah's identity as an Ethiopian and/or a Cushite.[9] The international edition shows a dark woman with wide nose and full lips, stretched earlobes and close-cropped hair (fig. 3.1, left). The North American edition shows her as a lighter-skinned, long-haired woman dressed in typical "Middle

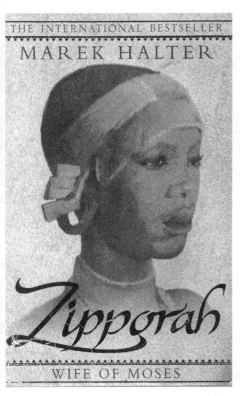

Figure 3.1. Cover illustrations for Marek Halter, *Zipporah, Wife of Moses: A Novel.* *Left*, international edition; *right*, North American edition. Random House Books.

Eastern" garb (fig. 3.1, right). Evidently different modern audiences demand different cover images for the wife of Moses; not much seems to have changed from the medieval controversies over Moses's wife's body.

Ham's Curse

Ironically, the story in Genesis 9 that is most often pointed to as describing the origin of blackness, Ham's curse, does not actually speak of blackness at all:

> And Noe, a husbandman, began to till the ground, and planted a vineyard. / And drinking of the wine was made drunk, and was uncovered in his tent. / Which when Cham the father of Chanaan had seen, to wit, that his father's nakedness was uncovered, he told it to his two brethren without. / But Sem and Japheth put a cloak upon their shoulders, and going backward, covered the nakedness of their father: and their faces were turned away, and they saw not their father's nakedness. / And Noe awaking from the wine, when he had learned what his younger son had done to him, / He said: Cursed be Chanaan, a servant of servants shall he be unto his brethren.[10]

Interpretation of the biblical account generally follows this line: After the Flood, Noah gets drunk one evening and needs the help of his children. His son Ham does not avert his eyes but rather sees his father's nakedness. Presumably for this reason, Noah curses Ham and banishes him. Part of the curse is written on his body to remind him and others of his misdoing—his skin is turned black and he will be the father of the race of Cush. Yet blackness is not mentioned in the biblical story. So at what point did Ham turn black?

Historian David Goldenberg has written a fascinating and wide-ranging study of the phenomenon by which the Ham of the Bible was blackened and made the forebear of black Africans, thereby justifying their slavery in biblical terms. Goldenberg's focus is on the Hebrew Bible and the origins and meaning of blackness in that tradition, along with its development through the ancient and medieval periods. He does not offer an exact date, but he finds a reference to Ham being blackened for his misdeed and passing that black skin along to his children in a ninth-century text.[11] It is clear that the transformation had taken place by the medieval period in Christian, Jewish, and Muslim sources.

By the high Middle Ages, black skin was linked with sin. In the twelfth-century *Voyage of St. Brendan*, the saint and his entourage land on an island where one of their group is possessed by an Ethiopian, as he is called in the Latin, or "Sathan" in the Anglo-Norman version.[12] Most devils and demons are portrayed as black in medieval artwork, building on an iconography that had been in place since the Greco-Roman period.[13] In fifteenth-century Spain, Moïse Arragel, a rabbi in Toledo, wrote an interpretation of the Bible designed to explain to Christians the ways that the Jews read and understood the Bible. Arragel's attempt at reconciliation of the two religions came just before one of the darkest moments in Jewish history in Spain—the expulsion of 1492. This magnificent text, replete with illuminations, includes an image of Ham and his brothers (fig. 3.2). Ham looks forward, facing his naked father, while his brothers

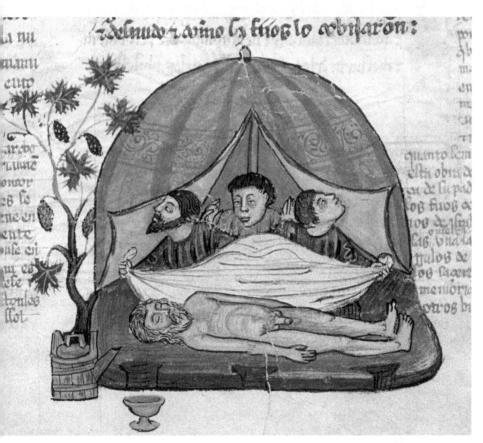

Figure 3.2. Noah and his sons: the curse of Ham. Illumination in a mid-fifteenth-century Spanish manuscript, the Alba Bible, folio 33r. Courtesy www.facsimile-editions.com.

look away and hold up a sheet. The artist identifies the three brothers with the races of Ham, Shem, and Japheth, using characteristic iconography of the period. Shem sports a beard and curls, Japheth is beardless and has straighter hair, and Ham has a wider nose and lips as well as tightly curled hair.[14]

The Arragel Bible image, found on the cover of Goldenberg's book, represents an iconic moment in the idea of "races" of mankind. The artist has depicted Ham, Shem, and Japheth with the immutable somatic differences that would become markers of race and has linked those differences to a moment in the Hebrew Bible where Ham has been cursed for his misdeed. Unlike the Saracen-Christian divide that so often appears in medieval texts, the brothers are separated by physical, not religious, differences.

By the fifteenth century—and long before—Ham, the black brother, was assigned to the area on the T-O maps marked Africa or Ethiopia.[15] Not only were otherworldly spirits given black faces in medieval art and literature, they were often called Ethiopians. A movement had begun to point a moralizing finger at black Africans as a group. At this point, however, room for positive black figures still existed.

The Queen of Sheba

The queen of Sheba was one of the most prominent and positive black figures in the medieval imagination. Known as Sheba in the Christian West, she was called Makeda in Ethiopia, Balqis in Arabic, and Nicaula by the Romans. Thought to have ruled the kingdom of Sheba sometime around the tenth century BCE, Sheba had a biblical encounter with King Solomon that secured her a place in the history and imaginations of cultures around the Mediterranean and beyond. In the Eastern and Western Middle Ages, stories of Sheba were amplified and transmitted throughout the Mediterranean.[16] Stories of Sheba appear in commentaries on the Jewish, Christian, and Muslim holy works.[17] She took her place in Boccaccio's pantheon of famous women, and Christine de Pizan provided a counterpart in her *City of Ladies*.

The biblical version of Sheba's story, told in virtually identical language in 3 Kings 10 and 2 Paralipomenon (Chronicles) 9 of the Douay-Rheims Bible, tells of Sheba's trip to the lands of King Solomon.

And the queen of Saba, having heard of the fame of Solomon in the name of the Lord, came to try him with hard questions. / And entering into Jerusalem with a great train, and riches, and camels that carried spices, and an immense quantity of gold, and precious stones, she came to king Solomon, and spoke to him all that she had in her heart. / And Solomon informed her of all the things she proposed to him: there was not any word the king was ignorant of, and which he could not answer her. / And when the queen of Saba saw all the wisdom of Solomon, and the house which he had built, / And the meat of his table, and the apartments of his servants, and the order of his ministers, and their apparel, and the cupbearers, and the holocausts, which he offered in the house of the Lord: she had no longer any spirit in her, / And she said to the king: The report is true, which I heard in my own country, / Concerning thy words, and concerning thy wisdom. And I did not believe them that told me, till I came myself, and saw with my own eyes, and have found that the half hath not been told me: thy wisdom and thy works, exceed the fame which I heard. / . . . / And she gave the king a hundred and twenty talents of gold, and of spices a very great store, and precious stones: there was brought no more such abundance of spices as these which the queen of Saba gave to king Solomon. (3 Kings 10:1–10)

Solomon never married Sheba, and the implied sexual liaison is not explicit in Kings or Chronicles.[18] However, the lover that is described in the Song of Songs (also known as the Song of Solomon) is often linked with the queen of Sheba in later folktales and commentaries.

Ancient and medieval historians peppered their stories of the past with vivid elaborations of bare-bones accounts gleaned from other sources. Flavius Josephus in his *Antiquities of the Jews* (book 8 chapter 6) tells the story of the Ethiopian queen who comes to visit Solomon, is impressed by his wisdom, and receives from him all that she desires, an account that follows the biblical story with little change. Soon following this, chapter 7 is devoted to a castigation of Solomon for having married many women of foreign descent.[19] By juxtaposing these two books, Flavius Josephus does not directly accuse Solomon of consorting with Sheba, but he indicates that Solomon had an inclination for exotic women, making the possibility of a liaison with Sheba well within the realm of believability—a possibility that was played out in the next level of "elaborations" of the Sheba-Solomon story.

The Ethiopian sacred text, the Kebra Nagast, was likely composed in the fourteenth century, though the dating is uncertain and the story of the encounter may well have a long oral tradition.[20] The central tale concerns Sheba, who was highly impressed with Solomon and stayed in Jerusalem for six months. When she informed him that she needed to return to her people, he realized how beautiful she was and wondered if he could conceive a child with her. He prepared a sumptuous feast with highly salted and spiced foods, and afterward he made her promise to share his bed. Sheba, a virgin, made him promise in return not to take her by force, and he agreed, provided that she not take anything from his house. Solomon had cleverly placed a bowl of water near the bed, and when Sheba awoke extremely thirsty from her meal, she drank some of the water. Solomon then held her to her oath, and slept with her, conceiving Menyelek, who would become the king of Ethiopia.[21] In modern Ethiopia the Christian Orthodox claim Sheba as their own. The royal lineage of Ethiopia up to its last emperor, Haile Selassie who died in 1975, claimed descent from Sheba and Solomon through their son.

Many medieval versions of the Sheba story are similar to the story as told in the Kebra Nagast. These focus mainly on the love interest and sexual relationship between the two rulers. The basic plot, of which there are *many* variations, is this:

The queen of Sheba has heard great things about King Solomon. Already a wise and learned woman, she decides to go and visit the king in order to test his wisdom and learn from him. She travels to Israel with a great retinue and bearing riches and gifts. As she goes to greet the king, she must cross a pool of water. She lifts her skirts to keep them dry, and everyone sees that one of her legs is really that of a goat. As she crosses the water, her goat's hoof strikes a log with powerful properties (it will eventually be used to construct the True Cross upon which Jesus is crucified), and her leg is transformed into a particularly shapely woman's leg. She emerges from the pool of water and greets Solomon with gifts. She tests his wisdom with a series of riddles, which he solves easily, and she is convinced of his wisdom and acknowledges his god. The queen stays with Solomon for a period of time, and she returns to her land pregnant with his child.

This story had, and continues to have, a powerful resonance across the Middle East and the West. Nicholas Clapp documents the long history of artwork—paintings, plays, novels, and film—dedicated to the meeting of Sheba and Solomon, and he also notes her appearance in Barnum and Bailey's circus. She even lent her name to an early twentieth-century American gold mine.[22]

Medieval audiences may have seen implications for contemporary situations in the questions of miscegenation, royal lineage, and universal redemption raised in the Sheba and Solomon tales. The mixing of the royal lineage of Israel (Solomon) with an outsider (Sheba) results in a union of the old with the new, and could produce an improved line of heirs to God's spiritual kingdom. However, any child from this marriage would have a mixed heritage, and if Western Christians felt that God had privileged their lineage, this could lead them to question the superiority of the West. A marriage has the potential of bringing legitimacy to a new regime, and this role gave black women an exceptionally difficult part to play.[23]

The Song of Songs: The Black Bride's Double Bind

An erotic love poem that never overtly names God, the Song of Songs was the subject of some of the earliest Christian commentaries—explanations that may have been needed to explain why the song was included in the canon from the outset.[24] A chronological examination of these commentaries points to a curious trend in views on the mixed marriage. The question of skin color and redemption was central to interpretations from the beginning. Symbolic or metaphorical interpretations of the bride and of the marriage are found throughout the commentary tradition, though some commentators made a point of saying that they saw no issues with a black bride. The woman in the Song is sometimes quite casually linked to the queen of Sheba, as we shall see with a few of the writers, while others do not make that connection explicit, if at all.

The early third-century theologian Hippolytus of Rome wrote one of the earliest Western commentaries on the Song of Songs.[25] His interpretation was that it was allegorical and typological. He saw the bride as representing Synagogue, or the Old Jewish Church.[26] The bride says, "I am black but beautiful," which for Hippolytus means "I am a sinful woman, but I am nonetheless rather beautiful because Christ has loved me." The bride as Synagogue has been burned by the sun, which represents for Hippolytus the warnings of the Old Testament prophets. The color of her skin results from burning words, condemnation that marks her as previously unredeemed and that she cannot rid herself of even after conversion.

Writing shortly after Hippolytus, in the mid-third century, Origen of

Alexandria began his phenomenal career as a writer and theologian. His *Commentary on the Song of Songs* was translated from Greek into Latin a century later and was widely available in the West.[27] Origen writes of the bride as actually being black and beautiful, though he makes a distinction between the black physical body and the beautiful interior (soul). But he also brings up other beautiful women that are black, including the bride of Moses and the queen of Sheba. He allows a very literal interpretation of black and beautiful, and in fact seems to prefer "brown" as perhaps a more accurate description of skin color. For Origen, the ultimate marriage was the marriage of Moses and the Ethiopian woman, because that united two peoples. He discusses possible criticism of the mixing of races, but finds instead that the marriage is privileged. Origen seems to accept the mixing of races, referred to as *genus* in his text.

Nilus, an early fourth-century ascetic and commentator, wrote in Greek and is believed to have lived in Ankara. His commentary was not translated into French until the sixteenth century, but his views may have spread in other ways, and his position may have been shared by others. His take on the story includes an actual whitening of Sheba's skin upon conversion. Like other commentators, Nilus goes through the Song of Songs line by line, considering each verse in detail, creating a commentary that greatly expands the original version of the text. Because Nilus extrapolates and interprets much more than is actually written, his (and other) commentaries become elaborate and fanciful, rivaling "literary" works of the period.

Nilus takes as his starting point the line "I am black and beautiful, daughters of Jerusalem, like the tents of Cedar, like the 'tentures' of Salomon." In a fourth-century version of blackface, Nilus takes on the voice of the black queen, writing:

> The black color of my base origin makes you wonder how I was judged to be worthy of the king because you think that you deserve it more than I do because of the nobility of your fathers. While my beauty may have been hidden from you because of my blackness until now, the Lord has seen it in my heart. Even though it seems to you that I am black because I carry the signs of my first condition, covering my condition like a fog similar to one coming from the stew of the idols, know however that like a tent, under my Ethiopian skin, an extraordinary beauty has been revealed that will be resplendent in the nuptial bath. Thus in the baptismal pool, when he who whitens like snow sins that were purple has washed me, I will emerge pure

and splendid, having gotten rid of my darkness in the water. And you who are now mocking me, under the shock of my beauty, you will become heralds and you will cry out to each other in wonder, "Who is this woman who emerges completely white?"[28]

The queen appears to be addressing Jewish women who are mocking her base origin, as indicated by her skin color. This harem conversation, both sides reported through the person of the bride, gives voice to both the Jewish and the black women. The levels of complication here are staggering: a white Christian Greek man is writing the scene, as he imagines it, of the confrontation of Solomon's soon-to-be favorite and the white-skinned Jewish women who make up the rest of his consort. Significantly, the queen immediately relates this to the questions of miscegenation and lineage. At the moment that the bride is whitened, which would then no longer be a mixing of different exteriors, the Jewish women will recognize that their blood relationship to Abraham does not make them the spiritual heirs to the kingdom of Christ. The queen informs them that "not all the sons of Israel are Israel" and that while they will continue to be of the race of Abraham through Isaac, the bride's children will be the children of the "promise." The queen offers an analogy, saying that it is like grafting onto an olive tree: one must cut the rejects from the base of the tree (analogous to the non-Christianized Jew) because their fruits are not the same as the graft, and the resulting tree will be more beautiful.

In the fourth century a seemingly small but important development in the history of the Song of Songs took place. Most of the commentators prior to this date were writing in Greek and working with Greek versions of the Old Testament, known as the Septuagint. The phrase in Greek at that point, as it was in the Hebrew, was "I am black *and* beautiful."[29]

The Bible had been translated into Latin, but unevenly. In the late fourth century Jerome was charged with the enormous task of putting together a definitive translation that would serve the Christian West as the official text. In the final version of this Bible, known as the Vulgate, the phrase was rendered "Nigra sum sed formosa" [Black I am *but* beautiful]. This would be the reading of the Song of Songs used in Latin for more than a thousand years. And when the Bible was translated into English, the reading in the King James Version was "I am black, but comely," while "I am black but beautiful" is used by the New King James Version, the New Jerusalem Bible (most widely used by Catholics today), and the New International Version.[30]

Using the Vulgate version,[31] another commentator, Apponius (ca. 410, location unknown but from the Latin West), considers as one all of the foreign women who converted and married into the Jewish faith. For him, they are the original black women of heathendom who lived in peace among these warlike, savage peoples. They are precursors to all the foreign women in the Hebrew tradition—Moses's bride, Sheba, Asenath.[32] The bride herself is a strange Medea-like prostitute. She realizes that she comes from a repulsive and fierce people who in their blackness and barbarous spirit are sometimes worse than animals. Apponius comments on the words *nigra sum*:

> She recognizes herself as black because in lying in the shadowy bed of error, drunk on the impious blood of idolatry, she suffocated many of her children with an eternal death. But beautiful because she sees with joy a multitude of sons, martyrs, virgins, and confessors around her that she conceived with Christ. It is she who, in the person of Asenath, prefigured her union with our Lord, the true Joseph, as well as in the person of the Midianite, wife of Moses. It is she who, as the queen of Sheba, came from the ends of the Earth to King Solomon to hear the wisdom of Christ.[33]

Apponius has created a grim tale around what some have called the greatest love song of all time. In this tale of drunkness and promiscuity, the bride, indistinguishable from all other foreign women, has few redeeming qualities. Her self-knowledge of blackness is linked to her memory of her pre-baptismal culpability. As a mother of many unbaptized children, she must forever bear the blame for having "smothered them with eternal death," rolling over them in a drunken sleep. However, she can rejoice in her new children, the virgins, martyrs, and confessors that she conceived with Christ. This black and beautiful woman epitomizes the Eve-Mary double bind, and it is written on her skin. She has damned her own children by her lack of salvation—through no fault of her own, though ultimately this eternal death can be blamed both on Eve and on her uncivilized "kind," who are born with black skin and in moral darkness. Once she is brought to the light through Christ, she becomes the Mary figure, the mother of the righteous who is, at least for some commentators, literally washed pure before her spiritual union with Christ.

These commentaries were some of the earliest that emerged from the new Christian Church by the very first Church Fathers. Early commentators saw these women, often treated together, as black (or brown, or purple, but at any rate with skin that was literally dark). The black bride could be washed white by conversion or she could be black and beautiful, but her skin color was a part of who she was and not always just a metaphor for something else.[34]

ॐ

Commentaries evolve over time. In the twelfth and thirteenth centuries, vernacular and secular literatures began flourishing. From this point on, new perspectives arose on black women in the Bible. While biblical commentaries continued to be important, literary works meant for different audiences and purposes were written by men and women outside the Church and copied and distributed through different networks. Monastic orders shifted practices and recruited new members to their communities, adults who had lived secular lives before taking their vows and who were familiar with secular love literature.[35] Ann Astell locates a shift in the commentary tradition in the twelfth-century renaissance, when theologians like Isaac of Stella drew on Augustinian principles that refuted Origen's Neoplatonic split between the corrupt "black" body and the redeemed "white" soul. In Origen's reading the perfected soul rejected the physical body, reaching out for a mystical union with God; Augustine affirmed the unity of the body and the soul.[36] As opposed to a Neoplatonic sense of a divided soul, an Augustinian view would be that the feminine is a lower part of the soul found within the soul itself. The feminine part lacks reason, acting through senses/love. Although it causes the downfall of the rational/higher (masculine) part of the soul, the feminine part alone will also be the salvation of the soul, because reason alone cannot lead to salvation.[37] The social and religious upheaval of the twelfth century necessitated a reconsideration of the Song of Songs, and indeed there was an outpouring of commentaries after centuries of neglect.[38]

During the twelfth century, Bernard of Clairvaux preached at least eighty-six sermons on the Song of Songs, with several of the sermons dealing directly with the color of the bride and the bridegroom. For Bernard the bride is black, but he must make a complicated argument to explain how she can be black but also beautiful: her blackness is due to her fallen state, but once she becomes the bride and Christian, she is no longer black. Interpreting verse 1:9, "Thy cheeks are beautiful as the turtle dove's," Bernard says:

You must not give an earthbound meaning to this coloring of the corruptible flesh, to this gathering of blood-red liquid that spreads evenly beneath the surface of her pearly skin, quietly mingling with it to enhance her physical beauty by the pink and white loveliness of her cheeks.[39]

Furthermore, he notes that many men are "black" because of their outward repulsiveness but we admire them for their inward beauty, and even the bridegroom is black before his redemption. Bernard makes everyone "black," including Christ, of whom he says:

He even brought this blackness on himself by assuming the condition of slave, and becoming as men are, he was seen as a man.[40]

Bernard does not truly address the question of the beauty of the black skin that the Song of Songs presents.[41] For him the blackness is part of man, like his feminine nature, that must be tapped in order to reach a low point. By thus debasing himself, man is able to become more Christlike and open to salvation.

With the emergence of scholasticism in the thirteenth century, Aristotelianism gained influence.[42] For Aristotle, as opposed to Plato, the literal sense of a text was as important as the anagogical, metaphorical, or spiritual sense. Nicholas of Lyra, writing in 1330, notes that Jews interpret the bride "a little too narrowly, saying that she is none other than the Jewish people and converts to Judaism."[43] Nicholas states, "It is the literal sense which I intend to present, to the best of my ability."[44] For Nicholas, the groom is God and the bride is the Church, "composed of different people, that is, Jews and Gentiles."[45] The first part of the Song of Songs is about the Old Testament, or old Church, and the second part is about the new Church. The bride at the point where she states "I am black" is the people of Israel.[46] So while Nicholas corrects unnamed Jewish interpreters who claim the bride as an allegory for themselves, he still sees the bride as representing the Jews, but only before she is converted, when she is black. After her conversion, when she is beautiful, she represents the Christian people.

Nicholas's commentary on the words *nigra sum* links a climate theory of race with the feminine. Calling the Jews weak for having lived a life of slavery in Egypt, he takes on the voice of the bride, saying:

I am black, that is, I am filthy in the sight of God, in the estimation of ignorant people, but in fact beautiful, O ye daughters of Jerusalem, that is, O you imperfect ones among the Israelite people, who are called "daughters" to emphasize their weak, feminine-like nature."[47]

Nicholas goes on to explain the origins of skin color, and he judges that a woman who is darkened is no longer beautiful.

> The Agareni, who are now called the Saracens, lived at that time in tents exposed to rain and snow in winter and to the sun's heat in summer. This blackened them on the outside, though they were beautiful on the inside. . . . Do not consider me, that is, for the purpose of judging, that I am brown, that is, obscure and abominable to God, because the sun hath altered my color, for a woman, beautiful by nature, if exposed to the heat of the sun, loses her external beauty. But such a change is accidental and affects only her exterior.

Blackness, Jewishness, Islamization, effeminate traits, physical deformity—these are the characteristics that Nicholas attributes to the old Church. Like Bernard, he is not particularly interested in speaking to anyone other than the white male Christian. He is not speaking of real people; those traits are valorized as the lower parts of the soul that will allow a path to salvation—the mystery of God's love that will allow access to the divine through abjection.

R. Howard Bloch, in his landmark study of medieval misogyny, characterized the alliance between women, Jews, and heretics as being on the side of the senses, as opposed to the side of the perceiving spirit, the rational Christian male who understands without the aid of the senses.[48] Bloch could easily have included Ethiopians and blacks in his list of those elided with women and non-Christians by commentators on the Song of Songs. While Bloch does not differentiate between Origen's Neoplatonism and Bernard's preference for unity, he explains the issue and the resulting problem quite clearly: women are forced into a both/and situation where they are expected to be Eve and Mary in one—seducer and redeemer.[49]

While Origen's Neoplatonic model, admittedly not a positive image of blackness, allows the black bride to be a separate entity with a corporeal body, models like Bernard's require the black bride to embody two contradictory roles at once. The black figure becomes so abstract as to have no meaning. By being a living contradiction, a part of everyone—Christ, the bridegroom, mankind—the black body of the bride is *no* body. Bloch argues that the contradictory role Christianity assigned to women robbed them of any true temporal authority in a paradigm of control and subjugation.[50] And robbing the external Other, the black, of a body was a step toward the "thinglikeness" that Dayan suggests is crucial for the slave trade.[51]

By making all pre-redemption peoples black, as Bernard did with Solomon and Christ himself, and Nicholas did with the people of Israel, these commentators create a link between Judaism and blackness, which is also gendered by its conflation with the pre-conversion Eve-like bride. These categories of difference—Jew, black, woman—can all be lumped together as one pre-conversion Other that serves as the counterpart to the Christian white male.

Despite the differences among these commentators, a few consistent points emerge over time. Physical blackness is linked with the lower classes and with those living in sunny climates, but on a spiritual or allegorical level it also indicates a pre-Christian or sinful state. Crucially, the "black *but* beautiful" formulation, as opposed to "black *and* beautiful," becomes ingrained in the discourse of the Christian West. When a woman hails from a culture where the people are known to be black, this creates a tension when she also needs to be beautiful to fulfill a function within the text in question: witness, for example, all of the "Saracen princesses" of medieval French epic, who are whitened in order to marry into a noble family.[52]

So how did the West represent Sheba, the archetypical black and beautiful woman, paragon of wisdom and powerful ruler? Despite the fact that she is repeatedly and overtly linked with the woman in the Song of Songs who claims to be "black but beautiful," Sheba does not appear to be either black or physically similar to depictions of Africans in medieval Western iconography. On Chartres Cathedral, for instance, Sheba is depicted as a typical Western female with an African beneath her feet (fig. 3.3), perhaps indicating her status as a ruler. In a fifteenth-century book of hours, a westernized Sheba in fifteenth-century garb crosses the water to greet Solomon, the plank clearly visible (fig. 3.4); a black figure in the retinue that accompanies her functions like the black figure beneath Sheba's feet at Chartres, pointing to her difference. In fact, Sheba is almost exclusively depicted with white skin in manuscripts from the twelfth to the sixteenth century, though her entourage varies and gestures toward her origins. While black figures sometimes appear in her retinue, as in the image of Sheba and the plank for the cross (fig. 3.4) or the image from a sixteenth-century Bible (fig. 3.6), her companions in figure 3.5 are classic hirsute wild men, part animal and

Figure 3.3. Sheba with African at her feet. Chartres Cathedral, thirteenth century. Photo by author.

Figure 3.4. Sheba crossing the water to meet Solomon. Illumination from a 1440 book of hours, with Sheba, attended by a black and a white woman, lifting her skirt to walk on a clearly visible plank that will become the True Cross. Morgan M917, page 109. The Pierpont Morgan Library, New York.

Cy apres senluit de xicau le royne des ethiopiens.

Figure 3.5. Sheba and her entourage of wildmen meet Solomon. Boccaccio, *On Famous Women*, BnF Fr598. By permission of the Bibliothèque nationale de France.

Figure 3.6. Sheba greets Solomon with black and white members of her retinue visible. Illustration from a 1540 Bible, Morgan M218, folio 133v. The Pierpont Morgan Library, New York.

part man. Sheba, with her amazing and unusual wisdom and virtue, must be seen as European, but her people in these images are clearly Other. She is acculturated and they are not. Metonymically these figures serve to underscore her uniqueness but also indicate pervasive questions about her origins, as she cannot ever fully escape her past.[53]

Literary treatments of Sheba also refer to her inimitability. The Renaissance humanist Giovanni Boccaccio, writing at the same time as Nicholas of Lyra, includes Sheba among the historical and mythical women in his collection *On Famous Women* (1374). Nicaula, queen of Ethiopia, whom he tells us the scriptures call Sheba, is remarkable precisely, Boccaccio notes, because she is from remote and barbaric Ethiopia and because her "splendid moral principles had their origin among uncivilized folk."[54] He goes on to tell of her descent from the pharaohs and her grand kingdom on the Nile. As he does elsewhere in the book, Boccaccio then points out just how exceptional Sheba is. She is unlike a typical woman both because she does not "abandon herself to idleness or feminine luxury" and because she is learned in the natural sciences. She is particularly to be praised because she recognizes Solomon's wisdom when she hears talk of him, and she sets out for his kingdom with an impressive retinue. She meets him, acknowledges his amazing and exceptional wisdom, and gives him presents. She returns home and is possibly, Boccaccio tells us, the first of a great line of rulers in her country. Other than being amazed by her learning and culture, he does not mention her background. He refers to her people as uncivilized, but he is stunned as much by the fact that she could rule as a woman as that she came from such inauspicious origins.

Christine de Pizan's *City of Ladies* and Boccaccio's *On Famous Women* have been compared by critics since Alfred Jeanroy pointed out in 1922 that almost three-quarters of Christine's examples are straight from Boccaccio.[55] Despite the title, Boccaccio's *On Famous Women* is full of ambivalent praise and details of sordid personal life. Constance Jordan notes: "In case after case, Boccaccio's accounts of the strength, wit, and resourcefulness of women are rendered deeply ironic by reference to feminine garrulousness, avarice, and lust."[56]

Christine's *City of Ladies* (1405) is a response to the misogyny of Boccaccio and other male authorities. Reason appears to Christine, telling her to interpret the negative remarks of the male *auctoritas* as "antiphrasis, which means, as you know, that if you call something bad, in fact, it is good, and vice versa."[57] Ironically, as Joan Ferrante points out, Christine uses Boccaccio as an authority, directing those who doubt the stories of Reason to verify them in his works.[58] Thus, referring directly to Boccaccio, she undermines his misogyny in a highly effective manner.

One of the techniques that Christine used to rewrite Boccaccio was to take one woman and use her in more than one part of the *City of Ladies*. Boccaccio writes only of ancient or pagan women, not including any women from the Christian era, as if to suggest that no women of his own time are worthy of praise. Christine's book is divided into parts based on the "type" of woman that she is describing. Unlike Boccaccio, she writes about pre-Christian women, Christian women of the Bible, and women of her own day. When Christine takes the person referred to by Boccaccio as Nicaula, whom the scriptures call Sheba, she makes two separate entries. She tells of Nicaula, empress of Ethiopia, when speaking of great women rulers of the past. For the most part, this mirrors Boccaccio's descriptions of the land over which Sheba ruled and her personal wisdom. Christine adds a few points, including saying that Nicaula was "profoundly learned in the Scriptures and all fields of knowledge,"[59] an amplification of Boccaccio's assertion that she excelled in the natural sciences. In addition, Nicaula becomes one of Christine's many examples of the single woman who excels despite her lack of a man, or as Christine writes, "she had so lofty a heart that she did not deign to marry, nor did she desire that any man be at her side."[60]

Sheba reappears in Christine's section on exceptional women, returning as a prophetess. Here Christine tells the reader that there are many women prophets, but that she will leave aside the Christian and Jewish ones because some might claim that the Judeo-Christian God may have given them a special gift.[61] Instead she invokes a pagan example, the queen of Sheba. In the first part of Sheba's portrait, Christine tells the same basic story as Boccaccio, relating the wisdom of Solomon as recognized by the magnificent queen who traveled far to find him. She tells as well of the gifts Sheba brings, which again reflect on the rich kingdom that the queen rules. While her ability to recognize the wisdom of Solomon, her willingness to voyage far to encounter this exceptional man, and her great wealth reflect well on Sheba, this section is really more about Solomon.

In the following section we learn what makes Sheba a central figure in Christine's pantheon of women. She is invited by Solomon to view the temple he built. On her way inside, she must cross a plank that has been placed over a mud pit. This simple piece of wood could not be put to a more undignified use—a plank that lies in the mud and is walked upon. And yet Sheba earns her place as a pagan prophet in Christine's city by taking note of this simple piece of wood, predicting that this very plank will be honored, since upon it will die the one who will put an end to Jewish law.[62] When the Jews hear this, they take her prophecy seriously. They bury the board, but miraculously the very same board will be found when needed for the Crucifixion and Sheba's prophecy will be fulfilled.[63]

Christine juxtaposes Solomon, who is astute but not sagacious enough to see that the wooden plank leading to his palace has a special, holy significance, with Sheba, who, though pagan, is endowed with a pre-Christian knowledge that surpasses even the wisdom of Solomon.

So what are we to make of Christine's rewriting of the role of this woman, and how does her portrayal of Sheba help us understand how medieval people viewed racial and ethnic difference? Let us look more closely at the origins of these figures. Boccaccio, we recall, says that Nicaula/Sheba comes from remote and barbaric Ethiopia and that she is a descendent of the pharaohs. Christine tells of the lack of laws, crude customs, and rude manners of the "savage" Ethiopians.

Both authors tell us that Nicaula/Sheba comes from the island of Meroë. "The island of Meroë" was, and still is, a phrase used to describe a part of the Sudan that is not an island but is land framed by two branches of the Nile and the Red Sea. This area was the center of an advanced civilization from 800 BCE to 350 CE, when the heart of the Egyptian empire relocated to this region. Meroë was best known for its iron trade but was also an economic powerhouse in textiles and gold. Its people developed a new script that replaced Egyptian hieroglyphics. Their government, though autocratic, apparently involved the sharing of power between the ruler and his mother, who was called the candace, thus giving women a vital role in government. Even into the fourteenth century, the area now known as the Sudan remained an active and prosperous trading center. While we do not know what knowledge of African history Boccaccio and Christine may have had, assuming total ignorance would be a mistake; Boccaccio had heard of a candace in conjunction with Sheba.

Both Christine and Boccaccio miss an opportunity to show Sheba's importance. Boccaccio says that Nicaula may have been the same as Candace, who was a great queen, and that the rulers after Candace, who used to be called pharaohs, were named for her. But Boccaccio, though referring to Candace as *regina*, uses the word *rex* to speak of the line she founded. He transfers the shared power between king and candace (or queen mother) to a single person, the king. Christine reverts to her stock notions that Christianity and rejection of sexuality are what empower a woman, thus obviating the possibility of the historical power that a real candace held—that of being the king's mother and coruler.

While Boccaccio and Christine differ on who holds the power, in the end no real embodied woman rules the land. Thus it is not necessary for either Christine or Boccaccio to address the black body question that plagued medieval biblical commentators. Both writers have already indicated that she is exceptional for having come from such a backward society, and by adding on to that her extraordinary abilities *for a woman*, Sheba has already assumed an inimitable and mythological role.

As one would expect from a work that focuses on the universal nature of female power, Christine's *City of Women* is illustrated not by portraits of individual women but rather by an author portrait and images of Reason, Rectitude, and Justice at work on the City; another illumination shows Mary leading the virtuous women into the City. Boccaccio's work, which focuses on the individual and exceptional nature of the women he describes, does include portraits of these women. One such portrait is found in a fifteenth-century French translation of Boccaccio (fig. 3.5). Solomon is seated on his throne, with Sheba before him. This particular image shows great detail, including Solomon's long and curly bifurcated beard. Solomon's skin is somewhat colored in the portrait in contrast to Sheba's skin—his skin-tone comes off as yellowish. There are no other marks of his Jewishness, though very curly hair was sometimes used to distinguish Jewish figures in illuminations. On the other hand, Nicaula or Sheba, from Ethiopia, is shown as a typical European woman with white skin.

The erasure of Sheba's blackness is significant, as Jacqueline de Weever has argued.[64] Sheba cannot be black, because blackness serves as a marker for the uncivilized and uncultured, and her biography argues that she is uniquely civilized and cultured. This intersection of race and gender provides a tension as insurmountable for black women as the Eve-Mary dichotomy for all women. In order to be exceptional and acceptable, a woman must be white, but that immediately means she can no longer serve as a model of black authority and power.

॰॰॰

While the Bible may not say much about race, by the close of the fifteenth century there was an established literary and theological discourse surrounding the few black biblical figures. Moses's Ethiopian wife, Noah's son Ham, the bride in the Song of Songs, and the queen of Sheba each played some role, small or large, in an increasingly precolonialist rhetoric.[65] Following the Flood, blackness was associated with a particular branch of mankind, the sons of Ham, who were cursed for his sin with their black skin. Black women, not unlike white women, were objects of exchange between men, but their blackness made them unsuitable consorts, often requiring a "whitening" either metaphorically through conversion or by outright erasure. Most significantly, when used as a symbol for Christ or as a path to salvation, the black body ceased to signify a corporeal existence, laying the necessary groundwork for the rapidly approaching Middle Passage slave trade.

4

Medieval Miscegenation and the Literary Imagination

Figurative mutations of skin color, such as the whitening of the queen of Sheba seen in images throughout the Middle Ages, were not the only way that medieval people imagined changes or varieties in pigmentation. We find examples of unusual skin coloring in many literary accounts, as well as in philosophical or theological texts that deal with intermarriage. When two members of different religions produce children in these texts, this miscegenation often manifests itself at the surface level of the skin. In stories that deal with conversion, not only skin color but even the form of the body itself can mutate.

Although medieval representation of difference on the surface of the body was neither systematic nor predictable, certain descriptions of skin color can be linked to medieval notions of hybridity and premodern ideas about genetics that point toward a heightened anxiety about which traits are inherited and from whom. Medieval people had little knowledge of internal anatomy or what occurred during conception and gestation. They knew still less about genetics, a field that would come into its own in the nineteenth century. However, they did breed animals and select crops and were consequently aware that certain traits could be passed along.

Medieval Theories of Reproduction

Medical science as we know it was limited in the Western medieval period. Medieval ideas on procreation and the transmission of traits often came from commentaries on selected philosophies from antiquity. One of the central questions for philosophers was whether reproduction required one seed from one parent or two seeds, involving both parents. Both camps had adherents. A third camp emerged that saw reproduction as a flexible process that could accommodate one or two seeds, depending on the relative "strength" of the seeds. Medieval literature reflects the importance of this debate, leaving us stories that center on whether inherited traits come primarily from one or the other parent, or sometimes from both. Children could inherit any number of attributes, from gender to nobility to skin color.

The one-seed theory is largely attributed to Aristotle, who saw the father as the sower of seed. For Aristotle, the mother supplied the body of the child, or the "material," while the father's contribution to his offspring was the soul.[1] In this version of procreation, the role of the woman in the outcome of the child is minimal. Women are viewed as defective men; they do not have the capacity to generate life but simply provide the physical space and the material from which the male seed forms the child. In the *Generation of Animals*, Aristotle describes what some have termed a one-sex body. According to Aristotle, the male body is the ideal, perfectly formed expression of the human body. However, the bodily fluids are not always hot enough to produce a male, and when they are not, a female is generated. As Thomas Laqueur explains, while Aristotle does not mention women changing into men when they are sufficiently heated, his argument allows for just that claim to be made by others.[2]

While the *Generation of Animals* states clearly that women are inferior variations of the perfect male body,[3] Aristotle does not make analogous judgments about variations in other aspects of the human body. He does, however, discuss hybridity and heredity in plants, animals, and humans. The philosopher has no problem with the concept of hybridity in plants. He writes of the vine that produces both black and white grapes. For Aristotle this is not a monstrous occurrence, as some of his contemporaries thought. The commixture of black and white grapes shows that different colors do not make incompatible partners.

Interbreeding horses and donkeys, however, gives Aristotle pause. The mule that is produced is often, though not always, sterile, which would indicate that interbreeding is of limited success. For Aristotle, breeding between completely unrelated species is not possible, so he discounts the notion that a union of a woman and a dog could produce a child with a dog's head. He allows that these marvelous events do occur, but he says they cannot occur from interspecies breeding. Instead he suggests that they are due to a problem with the male or female contribution to the child. Most likely, according to Aristotle, the problem arises with the material supplied by the female.

Aristotle's ideas on heredity stem from questions about the reproductive process, specifically the question of where the "seeds" that grow into a child come from. Aristotle says there can be only one seed, which comes from the father. But his theory falls short when it comes to inherited qualities. If there is only one seed, why would a child look like the other parent at all? Similarly, people noticed that at times a child resembled a grandparent or even more distant relative who clearly added no direct seed to the reproductive process. Another theory was needed to account for those characteristics, physical and otherwise, that came from the non-seed-donating parent and distant relations.

Galen, who saw his work as an extension and clarification of his intellectual predecessor Hippocrates, is the best-known proponent of the two-seed camp. For Galen, both men and women contributed materially and spiritually to their progeny. The Hippocratic tradition asserted that children were formed from seed contributed by both parents, seed drawn from all parts of the parental bodies. This process, known as pangenesis, explains family resemblance as based on the contributions of each parent.[4] Medieval thinkers had limited access to Galen's writings. Though some works and isolated citations were available in Latin as early as the sixth century, much of his writing was not available until the sixteenth century, when his entire corpus was translated into Latin. Nonetheless, Galen's Hippocratic ideas clearly influenced the scientific culture of the Latin West from antiquity through the Renaissance.[5]

Isidore of Seville composed his seventh-century *Etymologies* in order to preserve the knowledge of the past, including available texts from Aristotle and Galen, and to adapt that knowledge to the Christian experience. Isidore's *Etymologies* were read from the date of their writing until the end of the Middle Ages. A strong manuscript tradition of the *Etymologies* indicates that his ideas were available early on to medieval thinkers throughout the West.

Isidore discusses the possible outcomes of mixed marriages, though he specifically deals with marriages that are mixed in terms of power and class rather than race or religion. For instance, he notes that a child produced by a couple in which the father is noble and the mother is not will take on the characteristics of the father.[6] Isidore declines to decide the one-seed or two-seed question, opting instead for a third theory: the seed that produces a child is located in the father, in the mother, or in both. This combination of possibilities provides an answer to the problem of family resemblance. When intercourse takes place, the seeds of the father and mother do literal battle in the womb. The more powerful seed will determine the resemblance of the progeny. Isidore describes the process:

> They say that children resemble their fathers if the paternal seed be stronger; the mother if the maternal seed be the stronger. This is the reason faces are formed to resemble others; those with the likeness of both parents were conceived from an equal admixture of paternal and maternal semen. Those resembling their grandparents and great-grandparents do so since, just as there are many seeds hidden in the soil, seeds also lie hidden in us which will give back the figures of our ancestors. Girls are born from the paternal semen and boys from the maternal, because every birth consists of two seeds. When its greater part prevails, it produces a similarity of sex.[7]

Applying Isidore's theory to marriages between people of different faiths suggests that reproduction between a Christian and a Saracen or Jew could be similar to a *judicium dei*,[8] yet another battle between conflicting forces, this one taking place in the bedroom rather than on the battlefield. Medieval epic abounds with examples of Christian right doing battle with pagan wrong.[9] To follow the logic of the epic, one would expect that in the epic battle of the seed, children would take after their Christian parent, showing the superior strength of the Christian seed—and thus Christian thought—over the Jewish or Muslim seed.

However, not even in the most optimistic epic do Christians win every battle, even if they triumph in the end. The possibility of the "wrong" side winning in the battle of reproduction implies that children of mixed unions could indeed take after the non-Christian parent, particularly in cases where the Christian partner was in some way weak or flawed and thus susceptible to losing the battle owing to lack of moral superiority. In medieval romance the resulting child, if a child comes of the union, is often monstrous rather than a reproduction of the positive characteristics of the non-Christian participant.[10]

Miscegenation in Medieval Romance

All three views on reproduction and heredity find their place in Western literature of the thirteenth century. Medieval writers imagined the process in very different ways, some following the basic tenets of recorded philosophies and others using unique combinations and variations on known currents of thought.[11] Although Greek and Roman philosophies provided the foundation for how Western medieval people viewed parenthood and the biological construction of gender, the philosophical record is largely silent on the question of miscegenation or mixed-race offspring. Medical writings, too, address miscegenation rarely or obliquely. In contrast, the vernacular literature of the twelfth and thirteenth centuries seems particularly preoccupied with intermarriage. It is through these literary accounts that we can glimpse some of the ways that medieval persons imagined what happened when a man and women from different racial or religious backgrounds conceived a child.

Aristotle's one-seed view shapes events in the late thirteenth-century Middle English romance *The King of Tars*. A Christian king at war with a black Muslim ruler has a beautiful maiden daughter, said to be "white as the feather of a swan."[12] The Saracen sultan of Dammas hears of her beauty, falls in love with her, and agrees to stop fighting the Christian king if the king's daughter will marry him. She refuses, since he is not Christian, and a huge battle ensues. The Christian king's army is decimated, showing that right does not always prevail. Thirty thousand and seven Christian knights are killed before the princess decides that she needs to put a stop to the killing. She informs her parents that she will marry the sultan in order to save Christian lives. The king and queen allow this, and the daughter goes to the sultan.

At this point the narrator of the story provides an interesting bilateral view of the mixed-faith marriage, declaring it unacceptable to both Christian and Muslim societies. Just as a Christian man would be "very reluctant to marry a heathen woman," the sultan does not wish to marry a Christian woman.[13] The sultan instructs the princess in the ways of Islam while she feigns being a sincere pupil, and they are married. Soon she becomes pregnant. When the child is born, it is a limbless blob that does not appear to be alive.[14]

Jane Gilbert argues that the monstrous child results from the sultan's inability to impose a patrilineal line of descent in Aristotelian terms; the sultan's paganism prevents him from occupying a paternal position.[15] Gilbert's focus on the father, however, neglects the important role of the mother. Rather than showing that Muslims cannot reproduce properly or that the father is flawed, this formless child is an indictment of the mixed marriage. Had the sultan married a Muslim woman, the child would no doubt have been properly formed. Thanks to the child's lack of form, the sultan knows that his wife has never embraced Islam, that she has "false belief."[16]

The sultan places the blame squarely on the mother due to her suspected (and, in fact, actual) lack of faith. He misreads the clues: the child is indeed affected by the lack of agreement in faith, but it is equally his fault. The wife rejects her husband's espousal of a reproductive model that would allow a woman to influence the form and soul of the child; she can only provide material. She chastises him and reminds him of his role in creating the monstrous child: "Dear sir, let be that thought. The child was begotten between the two of us,"[17] and she sends the sultan to pray to his gods over the child.

Despite his sincere efforts, the sultan is unable to heal the child through prayer to his gods. When his wife suggests that they try prayer to the Christian god, he reluctantly agrees. A priest is found, who baptizes the child. Upon baptism, the child is miraculously transformed into a beautiful, perfect boy. After the christening the author notes that no child is fairer, that he now has all his limbs and is well shaped.[18] The sultan rejoices, but his wife cuts short his joy by denying that he has any part in the child's transformation, in essence rejecting his paternity.[19] While the wife earlier stated that both she and her husband were responsible for the deformed child, when the child is transformed, that part of the child that was attributable to the black Muslim father is no longer found in the son. Since the sultan is not Christian, the wife reasons that he has no part in either the child or in her. Along with the sultan's claims of paternity, the marriage that the narrator has already condemned is now declared to be nonexistent.[20]

The role of the sultan in this case follows closely Aristotelian one-sex notions of paternal agency. While there is a risk in conflating two very different concepts, race and gender, in the writings of the commentators on the Song of Songs the link between women, Jews, and blacks was made explicit. If medieval people were imagining gendered and racialized bodies in similar ways, then the one-sex notion of mankind that appears in Aristotle's writings on reproduction may shed light on what medieval people thought as they considered this story of remarkable transformation. For Aristotle the woman was a necessary, but always inferior, version of an imperfectly finished man. Aristotle's writings led to the belief that if the internal organs of women were properly heated, they could drop out of the body and transform what was once considered a woman into a fully equipped man. Stories of just such transformations were recorded from antiquity and the Middle Ages.[21]

Similarly in the case of race, the miraculous transformation moves the child from the inferior position of soulless heathen toward the more perfect, ideal Christian. Since it is the role of the father to supply the soul and form to the child, this child before baptism clearly has no form and thus no soul. It takes God the (literal) Father to provide the child with those attributes.

Though the union between the Christian and the Muslim appears on the surface to be simply a conflict of differing religions, the story color-codes the conflict. The daughter is said to be "white as the feather of a swan."[22] On the night the maiden is sent to the sultan, she dreams of being attacked by black dogs,[23] but she is eventually saved by Jesus, imagined as a knight dressed in white,[24] the dream thus showing a fear of both religious and racial miscegenation. While Muslims were commonly represented by dogs, the overdetermined blackness of the dogs reflects the negative connotations of black skin. When the child is baptized, Jesus—the white apparition in the girl's dream who saves her from the black hounds—becomes his father. Though the child has form and soul, they do not derive from the sultan, who would normally be considered the father, since only he has had sexual relations with the mother. This miraculous rebirth is made legitimate when the sultan follows through on his promise to his wife and receives baptism. At this point the miracle is doubled, for he not only regains his status as the father of his son but is also washed white by the baptism; his black and loathly "hide" is changed to white, fair and "without blame."[25] The poet connects skin color directly to moral stature: black skin is to be hated, apparently because it represents a fallen state, but white skin is morally coded as without blame.[26]

More important to the thrust of the story, just as the sultan knew that the formless child could only have come from a lack of belief on the part of the mother, the mother recognizes the genuine conversion of her husband by the external sign of his whitened skin.[27] *The King of Tars* is consistent in its portrayal of an Aristotelian-like one-race view of mankind; just as heat would allow a woman to turn into a man, baptismal water could change the color of one's skin.

Roughly contemporary with *The King of Tars*, the French romance *Fille du comte de Pontieu* offers a conception model more closely akin to Isidore's *judicium dei*. Like *The King of Tars*, the *Fille du comte de Pontieu* is from the outset deeply concerned with genealogy.[28] In the first folio it is revealed that there is a succession crisis in Saint Pol, where the count has no heir.[29] His sister has a suitable son, Thibaut, who will eventually inherit his uncle's lands. In the meantime Thibaut serves the comte de Pontieu. The count's wife dies after giving birth to a daughter, a potential crisis in a patrilineal society, but the count soon remarries and has a son. Thibaut is promised the hand of the daughter of the comte de Pontieu, a woman who is never named but is referred to only as the *fille*.

Thibaut and the *fille* suffer their own reproductive problems. After five years of marriage and no heir, Thibaut decides that a pilgrimage to Saint James of Galicia (Santiago de Compostela) would perhaps yield the much-desired result. Despite objections by her husband and her father, the *fille* insists on going on the pilgrimage as well. Before Thibaut and the *fille* can reach the shrine, however, they are set upon and overcome by brigands who rape her in front of her husband. Though the couple survive the attack, the *fille* attempts to kill her husband, presumably because he has witnessed her rape or failed to prevent the attack. When the *fille*'s father hears of her attempt on her husband's life, he responds by throwing her overboard in a barrel, effectively condemning her to death without actually killing her. She survives once again, saved by merchants who sell her to the Muslim ruler of Almeria, located either in Spain or in northern Africa.[30]

Like the princess in *The King of Tars*, the *fille* learns Islamic religious practices and even learns to speak the local language. Though a later version of the tale exists in which the *fille* fakes her conversion to Islam, the *fille*'s conversion in both of the extant thirteenth-century manuscripts is apparently real. The text does not mention any ruse on the part of the *fille* and states simply that she realized that she should accept the sultan's offer of marriage out of love rather than by force and that she renounced Christianity.[31] Because she harbors no internal conflict between Christianity and Islam, the two children she bears in rapid succession to the sultan are born whole and well formed.

When her father, husband, and half brother fall by chance into the hands of the sultan, the *fille* insists that they not "humble themselves before her" because she is "Sarrasine,"[32] a state that she evidently sees as morally questionable. As evidence of her genuine conversion to Islam, when she eventually returns to Christian lands, she must recommit herself to Christianity.[33] Moreover, the *fille* maintains a sympathetic view toward her Muslim husband even after she has left.[34]

An important difference between the two thirteenth-century manuscripts highlights the slipperiness of conversion and suspicions that surrounded those who may be weak or newly converted. When the *fille* tells her Muslim husband that she wants to speak to the foreign prisoners, in the first manuscript she says simply that she knows French and wants to talk to the condemned men.[35] In the second version, Nature seems to beckon to the *fille*, and though she does not recognize her father, she is somehow moved at his sight. She announces to her husband, the sultan, that she "is" French, an admission that should elicit some surprise, as she has never before identified her origins.[36] She spends time with her half brother, father, and first husband, and eventually discovers who they are.

Despite the importance of conversion and reconversion to the story, succession remains at the forefront of the text. The *fille* manages to engineer her escape, along with her three French family members, by feigning a pregnancy craving that requires her to return to her natural homeland, called her "terre de droite nature" in both manuscripts.[37] While the *fille* leaves her younger child, a girl, the Muslim-sired son who accompanies the *fille* back to France is baptized and renamed Guillaume.

With the *fille*'s return to France, questions of succession—the eternal preoccupation of the story—enter again into play. The count's son by his second wife dies, but Thibaut and the *fille* have two sons. As the oldest grandson, the Muslim-sired son Guillaume should become the next count of Pontieu, inheriting through his mother, the *fille*. Instead his two half brothers succeed as the counts of Pontieu and Saint Pol. Guillaume is married to the daughter of Raoul de Praiau, becoming lord of Praiau since Raoul de Praiau has no male child. While baptism converted Guillaume and may have washed him clean, it was clearly not sufficient to overcome his Saracen paternity.[38]

The departure of Guillaume to Christian lands with the *fille* creates yet another succession crisis, one that parallels the questions of inheritance that caused Thibault and the *fille* to go on pilgrimage in the first place. Guillaume's absorption into Christian society leaves the sultan with no male heir. Moreover, just as Guillaume bears the taint of his Muslim father, the *fille*'s daughter suffers for the actions of her mother:

> And because of this adventure, he loved his daughter less, who stayed where she was, and honored her less. Nonetheless the girl became very wise and grew greatly in common sense, so that everyone loved her and prized her for the good things that were said about her.[39]

Despite the *fille*'s conversion to Muslim law, a residue of Christianity remains ineffaceable in her daughter. The daughter is forever after referred to as "la belle caitive" [the beautiful captive] despite the fact that she has never known any other native land or law. The mother has passed along to her daughter a Christian inheritance that will always make her an outcast in her own society. This sounds suspiciously like racial reasoning.[40]

Continuing the parallel construction of succession problems, the sultan marries his daughter to his favorite knight, who asks for her hand in the same manner that Thibaut asked to marry the *fille*.[41] In the first manuscript the sultan seems all too glad to rid himself quickly of a painful reminder. In the second version, the sultan announces the girl's heritage with a certain amount of pride and expresses great concern for her.[42] He realizes that the knight is a good match for a daughter who comes from the most noble of French families. In this version the sultan sees her as his sole heir, and the noble seed of the mother is equally present in the girl's genealogy.

The text of both manuscripts continues to valorize the maternal seed: the daughter born of the union between the *fille* and the sultan will eventually be the maternal grandmother of the renowned Saracen knight Saladin. Saladin was one of the few widely admired Muslim knights, best known for his chivalric conduct with Richard I.[43]

Unlike in *The King of Tars,* in this text the color of the child and of his biological father are never mentioned, so there is no explicit contrast between black skin and white skin. Sharon Kinoshita asserts that the lack of color-coding in the text is due to the historical situation in Spain, in which Muslims were indistinguishable from Christians.[44] Jacqueline de Weever, however, has noted that the absence of color-coding can also be read as ethnic or racial erasure.[45] From the commentaries on the Song of

Songs and the stories about Sheba, we know that blackness can be commented upon, manipulated, erased, and even passed over in silence. The same is also true for other literary texts. While modern audiences often expect a character description including hair and skin color, medieval audiences may not always have had the same expectations. The absence of descriptive color does not imply that the character is *not* black or dark, a dangerously normative assumption.

When Western European medieval audiences heard stories about Ethiopians, Africans, or Saracens, what did they imagine? If a story about an African or Saracen does not mention skin color, which is often the case, what can we know about the ways they were mentally pictured? Many texts from as early as the *Chanson de Roland* do note color difference, and black Muslims are consistently seen as morally inferior. However, many Muslims are pictured as white or said to be white in literary texts. Studies in iconography suggest that while early artists did not distinguish Christians and Muslims in a battle scene—the two sides had identical armor, hair styles, and the like—by the thirteenth century a figure representing an "Ethiopian" or "Saracen" was more likely to be black than white.[46] This could suggest a shift in mentality in the late twelfth century, about the same time that Bernard of Clairvaux and others made the black body an abject part of the white body, a part that could never be a fully realized body of its own.[47]

But what of the third model of reproduction in the medieval West? Unlike the *judicium dei* model of the *Fille du comte de Pontieu*, the early thirteenth-century (ca. 1211–12) German romance *Parzival* by Wolfram von Eschenbach reflects a medieval view of reproduction that is largely consonant with the Hippocratic and Galenic notions of pangenesis. Book I opens with an introduction that goes straight to the mixing of black and white:

> If inconstancy is the heart's neighbor, the soul will not fail to find it bitter. Blame and praise alike befall when a dauntless man's spirit is black-and-white-mixed like the magpie's plumage. Yet he may see blessedness after all, for both colors have a share in him, the color of heaven and the color of hell. Inconstancy's companion is all black and takes on the hue of darkness, while he of steadfast thoughts clings to white.[48]

The conflation of blackness with blame, hell, and inconstancy leaves little apparent room for mixed-race marriage. And yet Gahmuret, the future father of Parzival, weds the black Moorish queen Belacane of Zazamanc in the early pages of the romance.

This marriage owes nothing to cultural acceptance or color-blindness. Despite the fact that Belacane is virtuous and without moral flaw, Gahmuret is repulsed by her black skin. The skin color of the people of Zazamanc is a source of anxiety throughout book I. Wolfram notes upon Gahmuret's arrival that he is uncomfortable around the Moors:

> Black as night were all the people of Zazamanc, and he felt ill at ease; yet he gave orders for lodgings to be taken. It pleased them to give him the best.[49]

Despite the extent to which the people of Zazamanc go out of their way to ingratiate themselves with Gahmuret and his men, the Angevins retain a sense of repulsion. For instance, Gahmuret unenthusiastically allows himself to be kissed by the governor's wife:

> The governor of the city then graciously bade his guest not to refrain from making any claim whatsoever upon his goods and person. Next, he conducted him to his wife, who kissed Gahmuret, little as he relished it.[50]

In addition, the queen's skin color is described as a potential liability for her relationship with Gahmuret:

> If there is anything brighter than daylight—the queen in no way resembled it. A woman's manner she did have, and was on other counts worthy of a knight, but she was unlike a dewy rose: her complexion was black of hue.[51]

In contrast, the queen's positive response to Gahmuret's beauty is unequivocally linked to his coloring:

> The great queen's eyes caused her grievous pain when they beheld the Angevin, who, being of Love's color, unlocked her heart whether she wished it or not.[52]

Clearly Gahmuret's whiteness is the standard of beauty not only in Europe but for the people of Zazamanc as well; the text notes that the people of

Zazamanc claim "they had never seen a knight so handsome; their gods were supposed to look like him."[53]

While Queen Belacane is never described as beautiful, she is held up as a model of womanly virtue. Before meeting Gahmuret, she loved Isenhart, who she implies would have been a more suitable match based on his skin color: "To all false conduct he was deaf, and in blackness of hue he was, like me, a Moor."[54] Belacane withheld her love while Isenhart proved himself on the battlefield, where he was killed before the two could be united. Interestingly, it is her love for Isenhart that makes her an acceptable match for Gahmuret, as this love and concomitant grief perform a metaphorical baptism of her soul:

> Gahmuret reflected how she was a heathen, and yet never did more womanly loyalty glide into a woman's heart. Her innocence was a pure baptism, as was also the rain that wet her, that flood which flowed from her eyes down upon the furs about her bosom. The practice of sorrow was her delight and the true instruction received from grief.[55]

This baptism is apparently insufficient. In the end Gahmuret abandons Belacane, despite the love he claims to have for her and the fact that she is pregnant with his child. He leaves her a letter saying that he is abandoning her because of religious differences and that, should she convert, she might be able to win him back. Belacane immediately agrees to convert, but Gahmuret never fulfills the promise of return.

Gahmuret contends that their mixed-race child is guaranteed a bright future if he should resemble his father, whose genealogy is filled exclusively with kings. In fact, the child Feirefiz emerges as bicolored, both black and white. The image of the magpie with which book I opened reappears at its end to describe the child: "like a magpie was the color of his hair and of his skin."[56] As with the magpie who set the scene for book I, the primacy of the white part of Feirefiz is underlined by the black queen herself, as "the queen kissed him over and over again on his white spots."[57]

The part of Feirefiz that was drawn from Gahmuret and distributed throughout his body in the form of white spots allows Feirefiz entry into the court of Anfortas and the company of the Grail knights. Despite being the eldest son of Gahmuret, there is no chance that Feirefiz could be named successor to Anfortas as the Grail king, a position destined for his younger brother, Parzival, whose mother is the Grail king's sister. In fact, as a heathen, he cannot even see the Grail.[58] Feirefiz ultimately receives baptism in order to marry the beautiful white Grail maiden Repanse de Schoye, leaving his first wife, Secundille, the queen of India, just as his father before him rejected a black wife in favor of a white one. As a Christian, now he too can see the Grail. His body, however, unlike the king of Tars's, retains its unusual coloring.

These thirteenth-century stories—*The King of Tars*, the *Fille du comte de Pontieu*, and *Parzival*—utilize radically different conceptions of the mixed-race child. The title of *The King of Tars* indicates that it is chiefly concerned with paternity, embracing the Aristotelian notion of the father; the other stories' two-seed notion of procreation provides for the possibility of inherited characteristics from the mother as well. While *The King of Tars* might appear to be the most racist of the stories in a modern sense because of its emphasis on skin color, the one-race view of mankind leaves the reader in a difficult theological position. White skin is valorized, but it is available to all through God's mercy. If mankind is all part of the same race and white skin is available to all through belief, this in some sense negates the possibility for racism and focuses instead on a universal community of believers. To return to the comparison with gender, the idea that women are really just men and that blacks are really whites could be interpreted as inclusive, advocating a redemptive possibility in which women can become men and blacks can become white.

At the same time, the assertion of superiority for the categories "man" and "white" contains the seeds of later forms of both gender and race bias. By holding out an ultimately impossible hope for redemption, this one-race view participates in the worst sort of oppression. In the two-seed or *judicium dei* models of reproduction, one racial or religious tradition must defeat the other. This model of conflict and battle can lead to the conclusion that annihilation is preferable to conversion and that the differences between the embattled seeds are so great that not only is complete conversion impossible—and thus the universal brotherhood of believers no longer obtains—but there are indeed different races.

Parzival is perhaps the bleakest of the medieval views on miscegenation. Although Feirefiz, in the Hippocratic tradition, exhibits spiritual and physical characteristics of both parents, black and white never mix to form a gray but remain distinct aspects of the individual. Moreover,

Wolfram makes it clear that black is bad and white is good. Although Feirefiz's virtues are recognized to the extent that he is allowed to become one of the Grail knights, he lives in a world that is separate from and will never be equal to the one his younger brother inhabits, until the moment Feirefiz converts and marries Repanse. A mirror of the magpie that opens the text, Feirefiz combines the praise of the white with the blame of the black, leaving the impression that all that is good in him can be traced to his white father, Gahmuret.

These differing views on reproduction, as embodied in three thirteenth-century romances, are not sufficient to indicate that specific people felt one way or another about mixed marriages and miscegenation. What they do show us is that there was no consensus about what happens when different peoples form physical and emotional alliances. While it may be tempting to see the Middle Ages as a color- or race-blind period, it is apparent that writers were attuned to somatic difference and felt a need to account for what happens when colors are mixed. Like Artistotle's grapes, the offspring of a mixed-race couple could be seen as a marvel of God's creation or a monstrosity, depending on the attitude of the writer.

Conversion and Taint

Religious difference was clearly an obstacle to marriage in thirteenth-century Europe. Even assuming one party was willing to convert, marriages between Christians and former Muslims were problematic, as there remained a sense that somehow the conversion was inadequate or incomplete. Converted persons, real or fictitious, remained under suspicion even after living in Christian communities for years.

The pathway to religious conversion depended on the gender of the person. For men, the ideal was conversion by logic. One example of such logical persuasion can be found in the disputations of the twelfth and thirteenth centuries, where a point of doctrine would be argued on both sides in order to determine the "correct" view. In one such orchestrated disputation, Peter the Venerable penned a mock discussion between a Christian and a Jew in which the Christian tries to convert a Jew by exposing the superiority of the Christian faith. The Jew remains recalcitrant, and the Christian despairs of convincing someone who, in his words, lacks human reason.[59]

Unfortunately, conversion by logic was evidently very difficult to obtain. For the most part, men in literary accounts were converted by force. Many an epic has a scene in which the hero attempts to convert a Saracen to Christianity on the battlefield using logic, only to resort in the end to killing the recalcitrant Muslim. Similarly, great literary battles of this period generally end with a scene of slaughter, punctuated with the note that only those who refused to convert were killed. This was apparently also the case in real life: as early as Charlemagne in the eighth century, and perhaps before, Christians engaged in battle gave their enemies the choice of adopting their vanquishers' religion or perishing.[60]

In Jean Bodel's thirteenth-century play *Le jeu de saint Nicholas*, the last scene provides an ideal example of this approach to conversion by force.[61] The Christians and Muslims engage in an epic battle that the Muslims win, at least initially. The Muslims capture a Christian and are ready to put him to death, when he begs for the chance to prove that his god is superior to that of the Muslims. As something of a game, the victorious emir allows the Christian to prove his religion by placing a statue of Saint Nicholas to guard the emir's treasury. Then the Christian god's power is put to the test: the presence of the essentially unguarded treasury is proclaimed throughout the kingdom. Robbers steal the treasure, but the Christian's prayer to Saint Nicholas results in the return of the treasure and the subsequent conversion of the impressed emir. At this point the emir demands that all of his followers also convert to Christianity or be killed. For the most part, no one objects to the conversion. However, one Muslim, the Emir d'outre l'arbre sec, at first refuses. He then announces that he will say he has converted, since he has been forced to do so, but that this conversion is external and not at all internal.

The Emir d'outre l'arbre sec illustrates an important point about forced conversion that apparently did not escape Jean Bodel—and surely others of his time—a forced conversion is highly suspect. One can never be sure whether the conversion has actually accomplished an internal change in the converted person. From a medieval perspective, a person's religious status—converted or not converted—was an essential component of the makeup of that person. Because religion was believed to manifest itself in the body, a change in religion could bring a significant change in the very composition of the converted person. As the wife of the king of Tars illustrated, conversion, while not always externally obvious, has a lasting effect on the makeup of the individual. The king of Tars suspects that his wife has not truly converted to Islam because their child is misshapen. When the child is baptized, he is physically transformed. So, too, his father the king changes from black to white when baptized. Internal beliefs and the external, even physical, aspect of an individual's makeup were not easily separated by medieval thinkers.

For women, conversion was seen as a response to gentle persuasion, most often motivated by the desire to become the wife of a man of a different religion. With men one would first try to explain the intricate points of theology. When that failed, one resorted to death threats. Women were not expected to have the rational capacity to understand theology, so that route was never tried. Threatening them with the sword was unseemly at best. Coaxing a woman with the promise of a better husband or life was generally the best method. Thus the daughter of the comte de Pontieu ostensibly converted from Christianity to Islam when she realized that it was better to have some control over her destiny. In the end, as we saw, she easily returned to her "true nature," Christianity, but her movements in and out of different religions were chosen, not forced, and related to making her marriage suitable, with spouses sharing a common religion. The same is the case for Bramimonde in the *Chanson de Roland*. The wife of the Muslim leader Marsile, Bramimonde is captured by Charlemagne's forces. Rather than forcing Bramimonde to convert, as he does the Muslim troops, Charlemagne specifically notes that he wishes for Bramimonde to convert "pur amor" [out of love] and gives her over to women in his retinue for training.

Perhaps a more typical story of conversion is that of Orable in the Guillaume d'Orange epic cycle, who converts to Christianity in order to be an appropriate mate for Guillaume.[62] She is motivated by tales of his military prowess. Despite no obvious way of knowing exactly what being a Christian might entail, Orable decides to convert and guard her virginity for her beloved, Guillaume. While Bramimonde might conceivably have been instructed in doctrinal matters by the Christian women of Charlemagne's court, Orable simply does not have access to any source of Christian doctrine. This lack does not seem to be in any way problematic. As women, it would be the exception rather than the rule if Bramimonde, Orable, and the daughter of the comte de Pontieu took any interest in the logic of Christianity.

Typical of thirteenth-century romance epic, *Beuve de Hantone* features a Christian, Beuve, marrying Josiane, a converted Saracen. This Anglo-Norman epic was quickly translated into Middle English as *Bevis* of *Hampton*, with some important adaptations. For one, Josiane's fair skin, likened to snow,[63] is continually underlined in the Middle English text. While Saracen "princesses" who marry French nobility are almost uniformly described as being white, at least in passing, Josiane's whiteness is central to her portrayal. She must be something of an anomaly, for the text takes pains to point out that she and Bevis seem to go together remarkably well.

Despite the fact that she seems well suited to her Christian knight, Josiane is tested over and over again to prove her fidelity and suitability as a wife. She is twice married against her will and manages both times to save her virginity. She also offers to save Bevis's life because, as the maiden daughter of a king, she is able to hold lions so that they will not attack. Josiane is expected to do much more than any Christian woman would need to do to prove her worth as Bevis's wife. As a converted Saracen, she is both capable of more than equivalent Christian women and also tested more than they would be.

Eventually Josiane gives birth to twins. She is unfortunately kidnapped following their birth and is taken from the twins, who are left in the cave where they were born. Bevis, looking for Josiane, happens upon the infants and seems to understand that they are his and Josiane's. He takes the children and hands them to the first two men he comes across, requesting that the strangers christen the "heathen" children and raise them for seven years, as he continues his hunt for Josiane. While indeed any unbaptized soul was at risk, the term "heathen" may also serve to underscore the Saracen origins of their mother. In the end, when the grown twins are reunited with their parents, the two boys are welcomed into the feudal structure. Guy, named after his paternal grandfather, inherits Hampton, while his brother Miles marries the king's daughter and becomes the lord of Cornwale. Unlike the Moorish grandson of the comte de Pontieu, their mixed parentage does not preclude their succession to their familial lands and title.

Because wealth and status in European society largely passed through the father, Saracen women were permitted to marry into important lineages.[64] Following the logic of medieval Aristotelian science, Saracen women could be perceived as acceptable mothers in important lineages because women provide only the material and men the form and soul. Therefore the truly "human" parts of the Christian human body, the form and soul, derive from Christians in these mixed couples where the woman is Saracen. Conversely, Saracen men were not allowed to marry into important lineages because they would father children who were Saracen in form and soul. Deviations from this model do exist, and they may indicate either a dual-seed theory, where the female Christian seed is able to overwhelm converted male Saracen seed, or an acceptance of the efficacy of conversion.

Gender roles in tales of conversion provide fascinating opportunities for us to reflect on medieval notions of heredity and religion. For the most part, men were converted either by reason or by force. (One would expect that conversion by reason would "take" better than conversions by force.) In fact, men in these tales seem to pass between religious states or at least affiliations easily, often in response to battlefield victories. For example, in *Gormont et Isembart* a Christian knight abandons his faith and follows the charismatic Saracen Gormont, only to repent at the moment of his battlefield death.

Women are rarely if ever converted by reason, most likely because reason was considered a male characteristic, while women were seen to be the seat of emotion and sentiment. Saracen women in these tales tend to convert following a pact with God (as in the cases of Orable and Josiane) wherein they will convert if they can win the hand of a particular Christian knight. This sort of conversion would at the surface seem to be much more fragile, since it is rooted in what a modern reader might deem volatile and irrational emotions, like falling in love with a knight sight unseen. Surprisingly, medieval literature does not indicate a wavering on the part of these converted women. Once they have committed to their man, they follow their heart to the end. By contrast, the Christian daughter of the comte de Pontieu has no trouble returning to the religion of her first husband as soon as he reappears.

Tales of Thwarted Miscegenation

Chaucer's Man of Laws Tale, written in the fourteenth century, gives a different perspective on medieval miscegenation. Custance, a Christian from Rome, converts two men before marrying them—a Muslim Syrian and a pagan Northumbrian. From a strictly religious point of view, both marriages are acceptable. However, the two marriages have very different outcomes.

In the case of the first marriage, Muslims warn the sultan of Syria that

Custance's father, the emperor of Rome, is unlikely to wed his daughter to a Muslim. The sultan immediately decides to accept Christianity for himself and the noblemen of Syria. The narrator presents this as a positive step, as indeed conversion of infidels to Christianity was high on the list of objectives for the medieval Church. As a Christian, the sultan should be a good match for Custance. However, the amount of time and energy that Custance spends lamenting her fate belies any true acceptance of the sultan as a suitable husband, a hesitancy echoed by the narrator. Fully sixty lines of the tale are spent explaining how and why Custance is traumatized by her impending marriage to the converted Saracen. These protestations and lamentations are rendered particularly pertinent when Custance later marries a converted "Englishman" with no metacommentary from Chaucer at all.

Custance is not the only person in the story to be horrified by her impending marriage to the converted sultan. The sultan's mother plots to end the marriage even if it means killing her own son. While Custance does not mention skin color, Chaucer draws our attention to the issue as the sultan's mother proclaims that however white Custance may be, she will be turned red by the bloodletting that the sultaness plots.[65] The sultaness carries out her nefarious scheme, killing all of the wedding party except Custance before the marriage is consummated, thus conveniently leaving Custance a virgin.

Custance survives the ordeal but is set out to sea. She arrives in another pagan land, England. Like the sultan and his nobles, King Alla and England as a whole convert thanks to Custance. Although Alla too is a converted pagan, Custance readily accepts him as a spouse and an acceptable father for her future children.[66] This second marriage takes place in a mere four lines (690–93) that contain no lament. Indeed, they emphasize that Custance is made a queen by Christ, suggesting that her noble marriage to the sultan was nothing compared to this divinely arranged match.

The second marriage is not completely unopposed, however. Chaucer deliberately repeats the vengeful mother-in-law story, with the significant difference that in the Northumbrian case the mother-in-law does not manage to stop the consummation of the marriage, which leads to the birth of a child. The mother-in-law's intrusion takes the form of a letter to her son, who is away at the time of his child's birth. She accuses Custance of being inhuman and tells him that their child is deformed because of his mother's deviant nature. The mother-in-law, like the sultan's mother, is successful in sending away the daughter-in-law who threatens her power and who has converted her son to a new religion. In this case, however, King Alla discovers the plot and summarily executes his mother. Custance and the child are later reunited with Alla, who discovers them unexpectedly while traveling when he sees a child who greatly resembles Custance.

By telling the same story twice but with different endings, the Man of Laws underscores that while both marriages should be acceptable to a Christian, conversion to Christianity is not enough to permit the marriage of the white woman with the dark man—or, as Geraldine Heng has put it, Syria "presents the prospect of a penultimate alienness, an alienation beyond the pale, by virtue of the race and color of its constituents, even when the aliens have been Christianized."[67] By contrasting the two conversions and marriages, Chaucer implicitly raises the question of what a child of Custance and the sultan would have been like. Would he still have greatly resembled Custance?

In France another fruitless mixed union forms the central concern of the Guillaume d'Orange epic cycle. The cycle begins with what some scholars believe is the oldest French epic, the *Chanson de Guillaume*.[68] The *Chanson de Guillaume* contains from its very outset the notion of intermarriage and cultural mixing, a theme that is carried throughout the cycle as Christians and Muslims intermarry and have children.

In addition to being perhaps the oldest epic cycle, the Guillaume d'Orange cycle is also one of the most popular, with various parts of the cycle found in multiple manuscripts dated across two centuries. The *Chanson de Guillaume* was first performed around 1100; the last episode of the cycle, *Renier*, was most likely written or performed close to 1300. The epic cycle developed as many epic cycles do: First the story of the central character, Guillaume d'Orange, was told in the *Chanson de Guillaume*. Over time, storytellers picked up on its popularity, developing the stories of secondary characters as they went. Orable, the Saracen wife of Guillaume d'Orange, appears in the *Chanson de Guillaume*, but she is much more fully developed in the *Prise d'Orange*, another text of the cycle that recounts how she and Guillaume met and were married. Likewise, her brother Rainouart, who appears in the *Chanson de Guillaume* only briefly as a giant working in the kitchens, was apparently so popular that he merited his own mini-cycle in the *Bataille Loquifer* and *Moniage Rainouart*.

What is striking about the Guillaume d'Orange cycle is that it included mixed-ethnicity marriage in its story line from its inception in the *Chanson de Guillaume*. The central story of the cycle is the struggle between the Christian ruler Guillaume d'Orange and the Muslim king Déramé. That struggle repeats itself again and again through the generations, but it always involves the incorporation of one of the enemy into the Christian family tree. Since miscegenation is a central theme of this important cycle, it provides us with a perfect vehicle for looking at medieval attitudes toward miscegenation and whether they changed over time.

In the Guillaume d'Orange cycle there are many Christian-Saracen unions, though all take place after conversion. The first of these, in the *Chanson de Guillaume*, sees Guillaume marrying the Saracen princess Orable, who changes her name to Guibourc following her conversion to Christianity. It is particularly telling that Guillaume and Guibourc never have children. In a cycle that is named for Guillaume and that is deeply concerned with the lineage of this illustrious family, the eponymous hero never continues his line. This may be in no small part due to continued hesitation about the character of Guibourc. She is indeed outstanding and courageous, but she also bewitched her previous husband.[69] She is even reported to have killed the children from her previous marriage or been complicit in their deaths.[70]

Failing to produce an heir himself, Guillaume is succeeded by his nephew Vivien. In the various stories that make up the cycle, Vivien is sometimes said to be the son of one of Guillaume's sisters and other times the son of his brother Garin. But in all cases Vivien is one hundred percent Christian. Both parents are Christians *de souche* (from the trunk (of the genealogical tree)—a French term used today to indicate ethnic purity—and Vivien could in no way be seen as tainted by Saracen heritage.

Nonetheless, Vivien himself acknowledges Guibourc's vital role as his foster mother. As Vivien repeats as early as the *Chanson de Guillaume* and again in *Aliscans* and *Chevalerie Vivien*, he is indebted to Guibourc, having lived with her for seven years. As he dies, his final words are addressed to this mother figure, using the term *nourrir* (nourish) to describe how she cared for him.

Although Guillaume and Guibourc have no children, hybrid characters do appear in the cycle. One of these is Maillefer, the son of the giant Rainouart and Aelis. From the outset Maillefer belongs to a different category of characters than Vivien. His father, Rainouart, is of Saracen origin but is never neatly categorized, especially following his marriage to the Christian Aelis. While the stories of Rainouart must have been hugely popular, given the existence of prequel or continuation stories such as *Moniage Rainouart*, his character almost always appears in a humorous context. Far from being an ideal convert, Rainouart's comportment during his *moniage*, a period in which he rejects the world and retreats to a monastery, makes one wonder whether he has any concept of Christianity. Indeed, his behavior is so churlish that the monks plot to rid their monastery of him. Set beside this questionable father figure, Maillefer's Christian ancestors are little better. His grandmother Blancheflor, Guillaume's sister, makes herself the sworn enemy of Guillaume at every turn. On top of this, his grandfather Louis is the ultimate cowardly king, making for a heritage that does little honor to Maillefer.

Through Rainouart and Maillefer, the intertwining of the lineages of the Saracen Déramé and the Christian Aymeri (Guillaume's father) continues for generations. Maillefer marries a Christian niece of Guillaume's. Their son, Renier, marries a Saracen woman. Renier's son is Tancrède, one of the heroes of the First Crusade. Tancrède follows the propensity of his illustrious family line and falls in love with a Saracen woman, whom he accidentally kills in *Jérusalem Délivrée*.

The treatment of hybrid characters in these romance epics suggests that societal acceptance of converted Muslims and their offspring was highly problematic. In the Guillaume d'Orange cycle, the main protagonists, Guillaume and Guibourc, have a mutually supportive and beneficial marriage, but Guibourc never completely rids herself of her Saracen past, and the couple, significantly, do not procreate. Maillefer clearly inherits many traits from his father, including his gigantic size, which proves fatal to his Christian mother during childbirth. Rainouart's descendants seek out their ancestor's culture in a very concrete way, drawn back almost inevitably to the Saracen people that Rainouart denounced.

The taint of the Saracen past never fully disappears from the line. The story of the lineage ends in a disappointing fashion for the listener who might have hoped for a happy ending. In the triumph of the First Crusade, Tancrède kills his Saracen love, and with her the prospect of continued cultural mingling. The cultural work accomplished by miscegenation has led to a dead end that does not bode well for Christian attitudes toward the assimilation of Muslims in centuries to come.

The romance epic emerges as a hybrid genre that tries to negotiate between the themes of annihilation found in epic and another possibility—cultural assimilation.[71] The death of the final embodiment of this idea, Tancrède's Saracen love, firmly situates the romance epic in a discourse that is masculine and Christian. The story of the lineage of Guillaume and his brothers, the sons of Aymeri de Narbonne, flirts with the ideas of powerful women and miscegenation between East and West, but in the final analysis one is left wondering what role a mixed-race person could truly hope to play in medieval France.

Ambiguous Conclusions

In the nexus of race and gender created by procreation (or lack thereof) between Christian and Saracen, medieval literary texts shed some light on early notions of race and potential origins of racial consciousness. Differing views on how procreation occurred meant that mixed-race offspring could take after the mother or the father, or could be deformed (or fantastically bicolored) because of their lineage. Procreation could even somehow be thwarted, presumably by incompatibility or divine providence.[72] While crusader kingdoms and commerce provided contact between peoples, literature provided a space for exploring possibilities—some optimistic and others offering no tidy outcome for mixed-race couples. In several of our stories, conversion seemed to hold the key to a happy ending for biracial couples (Gahmuret-Belacane, Guillaume-Orable, Custance-sultan), but in each case something prevents a fully complete relationship. Gahmuret leaves; Orable is barren; the sultan is murdered. These moments, in which shared religion is insufficient and the narrative is unable to overcome the difference between the characters, point to something insurmountable and inerasable: a largely unspoken sense of racial consciousness.

Not all texts and authors shared this pessimistic view of mixed relationships. Josiane and Beuve transcend a multitude of obstacles to be together, as do Aucassin and Nicolette. The king of Tars and his wife also live happily together, though their marriage is no longer technically a mixed-race one since he has been whitened. Then again, Josiane and Nicolette were always white, despite their "Saracenness" and despite overwhelming iconographical evidence that Saracens, in general, were pictured as black by the mid-thirteenth century.[73] These fantasies of miscegenation illustrate an anxiety, not necessarily a reality, about social and sexual intercourse between Christians and Muslims enacted in the safe space of a court performance or a manuscript page. Soon explorers would make that space very real, putting social and sexual anxieties to the test as New World encountered Old.

5

Mapping the Monstrous

Humanness in the Age of Discovery

While the medieval literary characters Maillefer, Feirefiz, and the blob-turned-child of the king of Tars illustrate anxiety about what sorts of offspring would come from a "mixed" marriage, they do not fully or systematically indicate what medieval people thought about inherited traits. Each character carries a somatic, or bodily, marker that can be attributed to doubts about one of the parents. Gigantic size, piebald skin, and blackness coupled with physical defect are outward signs of their dubious nature. Such concerns were not suddenly put to rest when Columbus sailed or even when Montaigne and Shakespeare took up their pens. If anything, anxiety about the unknown and the people inhabiting it increased with the Age of Discovery.

Sixteenth-century European explorers looked westward to new lands and new resources, but they viewed the peoples they encountered through the filter of ancient and medieval travel accounts. Like earlier voyagers, Renaissance travelers were fascinated by the physical and social differences of the peoples they met. They looked for ways to describe the men and women they came upon. More often than not, and particularly in the very first reports, they followed the medieval models that they had inherited. Medieval travelers, themselves borrowing from Roman accounts, categorized the peoples they met based on physical and social customs, describing "races" of men that were later referred to as the "monstrous races." Verbal accounts of these races, accompanied at times with illustrations or depictions of these peoples on period maps, show a great deal of continuity between medieval travelers and the first Europeans to describe the Americas. These depictions appeared not only in travel accounts but also in literary works of imagined travel, such as Rabelais's *Tiers Livre* and Shakespeare's *The Tempest*. Over time, they became became an integral part of the European imagination of the Other.

As Europeans later wrestled with the problem of the status of New World peoples in European society, they drew on thirteenth-century debates about whether monstrous peoples could actually be considered human. Frank Lestringant states, "If, for example, [Renaissance cartographers depicted] monstrous populations inherited from Pliny, St. Augustine and Isidore of Seville, it was only in order to establish provisional boundaries for a knowledge in a perpetual state of progress."[1] For Lestringant, the monstrous races are put on maps to show the limits of knowledge, acting as indications of the farthest reaches of discovery, much like the crosses erected by early modern explorers to mark their passage through new territory.[2] Lestringant argues that, rather than building on earlier travel accounts, Renaissance travelers turned their backs on the Middle Ages.[3] To the contrary, not only were Renaissance explorers indebted to their medieval forebears—Christopher Columbus used both Mandeville and Marco Polo as references for his own travels[4]—but they had great difficulty interpreting the world through any other lens.

Are Monsters Men? Medieval Perspectives

The story of the "monstrous races" begins in the first century of the Common Era with the entertaining accounts of the Roman sea captain Pliny the Elder. Pliny's *Natural History* is a compilation of the encyclopedic knowledge of his time, augmented by his own insight as a traveler and keen observer. His *Natural History* has been popular ever since the time of its writing, and excerpts from the ten-volume Loeb edition are frequently required course reading almost two thousand years after Pliny's death. Pliny was not the only writer to describe the monstrous races, but due to the liveliness of his accounts and the vagaries of which ancient texts survived, medieval and early modern writers refer almost exclusively to his accounts, citing Pliny by name and calling marvelous peoples "Plinian races." In *Natural History*, Pliny catalogues forty-odd peoples with attributes from cannibalism to excessive hairiness, from those sporting a dog's head to those with no discernable head, just eyes and a mouth in their chests. Just as Pliny celebrated a wide assortment of basic physical properties of animals, minerals, and plants, so he found these races to show the diversity of mankind.

These peoples were wonderful illustrations of the marvels produced by the natural world.

Medieval thinkers, inheriting Pliny's fascination with prodigies and wonders, interpreted the place of the monstrous races in the order of things in radically different ways. The concept of the Great Chain of Being (fig. 5.1), an idea medieval thinkers took from the classical period and passed on to later periods, is perhaps the most common way of understanding how medieval Westerners classified people and things.[5] According to this widely accepted idea, everyone and everything in existence has a place on the chain, visualized as extending from Heaven to Hell. God stands at the top of the chain, followed by the angels and heavenly host. In rough categories, man, then the beasts, then plants, and even minerals have their place extending down into the Earth, where Dante places Lucifer and his cohort at the bottom of the chain. Alternatively, in many pictorial representations the fallen angels appear not to be on the chain at all. In addition to the major groupings on the chain, each individual part of creation has a relative position based on its being closer to or farther from divine perfection. Thus gold would be placed above silver, man above woman, king above commoner. While most variations of the chain do not specify in great detail what belongs where, the question of where to place the monstrous races clearly preoccupied medieval thinkers. Were these races men or beasts?

Adding urgency to that question, the idea that God intended for all mankind to be saved also shaped the discourse on monstrous races. The ideal of the "universal church," a Christian church whose message of salvation was available to and aimed at all, dominated Christian thought early on. Universalism puts a heavy onus on Christians, since the possibility for all to be saved rests entirely on access to the truth of the Gospel. Separate from the beasts, man alone has the capacity to reason, understand, and embrace Christianity's message. A necessary corollary of universalism is that while salvation is available to all men, it is denied to all who are not men, those who are incapable of receiving the message. Clearly beasts are not men, but the humanness of others—women, Jews, blacks—has sometimes been called into question.

Thus it comes as no surprise that one of the most popular questions surrounding Plinian races was whether they could be considered men or not. Augustine of Hippo (d. 386) raises the problem in his chapter of the *City of God* (*De Civitate Dei*) titled "Whether Certain Monstrous Races

Figure 5.1. The Great Chain of Being, showing the relative positions of all things. Didacus Valads, *Rhetorica Christiana*.

of Men Are Derived from the Stock of Adam or Noah's Sons."[6] Augustine employs Pliny's catalog of the monstrous races, but he adds the Christian concern that would become the focus of increasing anxiety concerning these races in the medieval period: how do the monstrous races fit into God's plans for mankind? Augustine finds that any being that can be considered a man is capable of salvation. He reasons that since monstrous births (deformities) occur even in his own society, there can be no question but that the monstrous races are also descended from Adam. We see their appearances as a fear-provoking deviation from humankind, but for God they are a part of his plan and not monstrous at all. From Augustine's treatment of the topic, we see that the question was already under discussion in certain circles before the medieval period—and that his answer is noncommittal:

> It is asked whether we are to believe that certain monstrous races of men, spoken of in secular history, have sprung from Noah's sons, or rather, I should say, from that one man from whom they themselves were descended. . . . But whoever is anywhere born a man, that is, a rational, mortal animal, no matter what unusual appearance he presents in color, movement, sound, nor how peculiar he is in some power, part, or quality of his nature, no Christian can doubt that he springs from that one protoplast. . . . All the races which are reported to have diverged in bodily appearance from the usual course which nature generally or almost universally preserves, if they are embraced in that definition of man as rational and mortal animals, unquestionably trace their pedigree to that one first father of all. . . . It ought not to seem absurd to us that as in individual races there are monstrous births, so in the whole race there are monstrous races. Wherefore, to conclude this question cautiously and guardedly, either these things which have been told of some races have no existence at all; or if they do exist, they are not human races; or if they are human, they are descended from Adam.[7]

If they even exist, which is in doubt, and if they are men (defined as rational and mortal), the monstrous races must be descended from Adam. Rationality is a defining characteristic of humanness, but Augustine does not attempt to determine whether monstrous peoples are capable of reason; rational thinking is a test that will become central to later discussions of other races and their humanness.

Bridging the gap between the ancient and the medieval worlds, the encyclopedic *Etymologiae* (*Etymologies*) of Isidore of Seville (560–636) was perhaps the most often used source for general knowledge in the medieval West. Isidore believed that groups of people are constituted by the language they speak, following the confusion of tongues at the Tower of Babel.[8] According to Isidore, the grouping of peoples is based not on religion but rather on whether they are descendants of Japheth, Ham, or Shem; a complicated interrelationship of language and genealogy determines the *gens* to which one belongs.[9] From these three main branches begun by Noah's sons, the various subcategories of people are grouped based on their language. Physically, mankind differs according to the climate: "The physical aspect of men, their color, their bodies, and the diversity of their temperaments is dependent on the various climates. Thus we see truly that Romans are serious, Greeks are shallow, Africans are 'versatile' [versipelles], the Gauls are of a proud and vicious spirit, according to the nature of the climates."[10] Later in the chapter Isidore underlined the fact that "Moors" (Maurus) are so named because they are black, and their blackness comes from the heat of the sun.[11] Despite the varieties of mankind descended from Noah's three sons, Isidore had no doubt that all of mankind is related through Noah.[12]

Of all the Plinian races, the pygmies attract more interest than their variation from any norm might suggest. Pliny simply noted that they are quite small and that they hunt crane eggs so that the adult cranes will not attack them.[13] The thirteenth-century theologian Albertus Magnus took up the question of pygmies in his *De animalibus*, writing:

> The Pygmy is the most perfect of animals. Among all the others, he makes most use of memory and most understands by audible signs. On this account he imitates reason even though he truly lacks it. Reason is the power of the soul to learn through experience out of past memories and through syllogistic reasoning, to elicit universals and apply them to similar cases in matters of art and learning. This, however, the Pygmy cannot do; the sounds he takes in by his ear, he cannot divide into sound and meaning. Though the Pygmy seems to speak, he does not dispute from universals, but rather his words are directed to the particulars of which he speaks. Thus, the cause of his speech is as a shadow resulting from the sunset of reason. Reason is twofold. One part is its reflection of the particulars of sense experience and memory, the other the universals derived

from the particulars of the first part, which is the principle of all art and learning. The Pygmy does not have even the first of these two parts of reason, and so does not have even the shadow of reason. Accordingly, he perceives nothing of the quiddities of things, nor can he comprehend and use the figures of logical argumentation.[14]

Albert laid out one of the essential problems for determining whether a being is a man or not: does he speak with reason, or does his speech simply relate to everyday activities? The higher-level capacity for reasoning is given only to those God has determined to be "human," so when Western travelers encounter beings who appear to be human and may even possess language, if that language is not sufficiently rational, then those beings cannot be men.

In 1301 a Parisian canon named Peter of Auvergne weighed in on the ongoing debate "Are pygmies men?"[15] Though he made a case for the humanness of pygmies, Peter's writing on this topic fortunately includes a point-by-point refutation of the arguments used for claiming nonhuman status for pygmies, thus giving insight into the reasons medieval philosophers may have offered for claiming superiority to these short-statured people. The arguments countered by Peter of Auvergne include the claim that while pygmies may look the same as men, they do not have the same quantity of matter and thus cannot be men. More telling, Peter's quodlibet indicates that there is already a question of whether the pygmies are actually descended from Adam.[16]

By focusing attention on pygmies, and describing them in ways that generally focus on the superficial characteristic of height, Isidore and Peter force their readers to think of themselves in smaller versions. As opposed to arguing the humanity of a cynocephalus, which would require the reader to identify with something very foreign and perhaps distasteful, thinking of oneself in miniature does not or should not bring about any sort of revulsion. It is in the writings of Albertus Magnus that we see an argument that truly questions the worth of the pygmy: if the pygmy cannot reason, then the pygmy is no longer human.

Medieval Verbal and Pictorial Accounts of the World

While Pliny the Elder described his encounters with the wonders of new worlds and peoples he discovered on his voyages, most medieval accounts of the world were not firsthand. On the basis of the stories they read and facts gathered from various sources, medieval people wrote about worlds they had not seen and made maps of imagined lands. Unlike later maps, which depict the relative physical location of geographical places, the standard medieval map depicts a Christian vision of the world. Many of them also illustrate how monstrous races fit into medieval concepts of grace and salvation.

Medieval maps were often T-O maps, in which the O shape of the world is divided by T-shaped bodies of water into sectors—Asia, Europa, and Africa—with the East oriented to the top of the map. In general, the monstrous races were placed at the edge of the Earth, in the unknown and unvisited regions of Africa and Asia. In one variation, on the wonderfully detailed fourteenth-century Hereford *mappamundi*, the largest extant medieval map, the monstrous races can be found along the far right side, south of the Christian West, in the margins of the known world. Mapmakers seemed unsure of what to do with the monstrous races on this physical and yet also spiritual map.

Part of the reason for their lack of confidence relates back to the unsettled place that these races held for the Christian faith. As Augustine had noted, if they were men, then they should, or could, be Christianized. For medieval thinkers, the physical space of the world held spiritual significance, so the placement of peoples on the map would indicate their relationship to the Gospel: whether or not they had yet had the opportunity to hear God's word. The implicit relationship between geography and spiritual qualities that underlies medieval T-O maps is made explicit in Hugh of Saint-Victor's *De arca Noe mistica* (On the mystical interpretation of Noah's Ark), written around 1130. Professor at the illustrious school of Saint-Victor in Paris, Hugh created a mental image of the basic medieval map of the world, and he assigned spiritual qualities to the various parts and peoples of the globe. His verbal map is a record of salvation history, showing how divine grace moved from the East to the West:

> The first man was placed in the East from his creation and from this original point his descendants must cover the Earth. . . . Then the center moved toward Greece, before supreme power then descended near the end of time to the West, to the Romans, who live in a way at the end of the world.[17]

The link to salvation is repeated in the framework of the entire *mappamundi*. Hugh has located the earthly paradise, the Garden of Eden, at the top (eastern extreme) of the map, and he places the Last Judgment at the bottom, in the westernmost sector. At the Last Judgment an avenging angel separates the two groups of the righteous and the damned. This sense that God's grace has moved from east to west, combined with the onus of enlightening the ignorant that is placed on those who have been exposed to the Truth,[18] would have important ramifications for New World explorers.

Medieval Accounts of Exotic Lands

Theologians debated the humanity of the Plinian races, but few questioned their existence. They were treated as factual in the encyclopedic compilations of knowledge that were popular at the time, most notably in Bartholomaeus Anglicus's *De proprietatibus rerum* (*On the Properties of Things*), an encyclopedia of medieval knowledge treating everything from God and the angels to gemstones and geography and the human body, written around 1240.

Very little is known about Bartholomew. He is mentioned in a chronicle by 1230, and his writings on elephants are referred to by Salimbene of Parma in 1284.[19] His sources are the usual panoply of medieval authorities, including Albertus Magnus, Isidore of Seville, Augustine of Hippo, Pliny, and Aristotle. Bartholomew also included Greek and Arabic sources that had recently become available in new translations. Because of his wide-ranging sources, Bartholomew's encyclopedia was one of the most popular reference books of the Middle Ages. More than a hundred manuscripts still survive. The Sorbonne made a chained copy available for general use, a sure sign that the book was popular enough that it risked being stolen. The encyclopedia remained popular after the advent of printing, with eighteen editions and translations into French, English, Provençal, Dutch, Spanish, and Italian in the early years of printing.[20]

Following Pliny for the most part, Bartholomew notes several types of monstrous men, including cave-dwelling troglodytes, couples that live together without marriage, naked men, and the headless blemmye, who have eyes in their chests. Tellingly, Bartholomew includes the monstrous men twice in his encyclopedia, once under the categories of men and again under the rubric of animals.[21] He seems to have trouble deciding whether these almost-men count as men.

While Bartholomew did not claim to travel himself, even those who actually did travel tended to follow the descriptions of the encyclopedists, embellishing their firsthand accounts with stories of the monstrous races. Odoric of Pordenone, a Franciscan monk born not far from Venice, apparently undertook travels between 1317 and 1330 for the purpose of converting those he encountered, following in the footsteps of four Franciscan friars who had been martyred in the East. Odoric's route took him from Italy through Turkey, Iraq, and Iran and onward to the coast of India. From there he sailed east, stopping in at the island lands of Sri Lanka, Sumatra, and Borneo on his way up the coast of China.

Odoric does not always comment on the physical appearance of the peoples he encounters, but if they are very unusual, he mentions it. At the island of Nicoveran, he reports on people who are dog-faced, the cynocephali.[22] He notes that they worship oxen and wear a gold or silver ox on their forehead in honor of their god. Odoric clearly considers these to be people capable of religious belief, albeit odd. Indeed, Odoric claims that the king "attends to justice and maintains it, and throughout his realm all men may fare safely."[23]

Odoric find the cynocephali undeniably human, but he is less certain about the humanity of other races that he meets on his voyages. The nakedness that Odoric finds among certain peoples raises questions about their humanity, for clothing is one of the hallmarks of humanness, according to Augustine and Hugh of Saint-Victor.[24] Likewise, the cross between animal and human poses problems for Odoric, with one example being his visit to the "monastery of idolators" in Manzi. Wanting to show Odoric a memorable sight, a Christian convert takes Odoric to a secluded area and bangs a gong. Odoric describes a "multitude of animals" that descend from a hill in order to be fed table scraps by the convert. They are "apes, monkeys, and many other animals having faces like men, to the number of some three thousand," who "took up their places round him in regular ranks."[25] When they were fed and had left, the convert explains that they are the souls of gentlemen, charitably fed in honor of God's love. Odoric denies this, saying, "No souls be these, but brute beasts of sundry kinds."[26] The convert insists, but Odoric is not swayed.

Odoric's interpretation of the cultures of the cynocephali and the animals with faces like men is picked up by the fifteenth-century illuminations of Odoric's text found in the manuscript BnF fr. 2810. Trappings of Western culture appear in the image of the cynocephali (fig. 5.2), including elements that point to the cynocephali's ability to reason. They wear

Figure 5.2. The cynocephali of Odoric of Pordenone. *Livre des merveilles*, 1:92.

clothing, an indication that they are postlapsarian and possess the ability to be ashamed of their own naked bodies. They presumably have built the town in which they dwell, and one of the cynocephali, apparently a guard, carries a spear. Outside the walls, the cynocephali are performing some sort of work, and their gestures indicate that they are communicating with each other. The elaborate headdresses that they wear are interpretations of Odoric's mention of a religious belief involving bovine veneration, and the king is clearly discernable by his authoritative posture, scepter, and dress.

In stark contrast, the human-faced sheep that appear in the same manuscript (fig. 5.3) clearly do not possess reason. While the text describes many different types of animals at the monastery of idolators in Manzi, the illumination of this scene is filled with human-faced sheep, perhaps because man-faced apes would be too much like the humans depicted. Enclosed in a penlike area within the walls of a city clearly built by the men in the image, the sheep show no signs of communicating either among themselves or with their keepers. Elsewhere in Odoric's text, the difficulty of distinguishing between animal and human

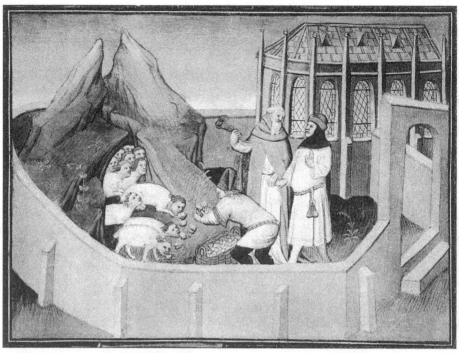

Figure 5.3. The human-faced sheep of Odoric of Pordenone. *Livre des merveilles*, 1:97.

Figure 5.4. The hybrid melon-lamb of Jean de Mandeville. *Livre des merveilles*, 2:179.

spills over into the problem of separating animal and vegetable. Odoric (echoed by John Mandeville) tells of a certain melon that, when open, contains a small lamb and is thus both fruit and meat in one.[27]

Though these hybrids pose a problem, Odoric is unequivocal when he visits the pygmies: "These Pygmies, both male and female, are famous for their small size. But they have rational souls like ourselves."[28] Had Odoric seen a superficial physical characteristic such as size (or skin color) as an impediment to salvation, that would constitute racism, but at least in this case, counter to Albertus Magnus's assertion, we see that the rational soul is not denied to the pygmy.

Mandeville's Travels and the Curse of Ham

In the mid-fourteenth century, one of the most enduringly popular and charming travel accounts of the European Middle Ages began to circulate throughout the West. By the end of the century it had been translated into every major European language. Jean de Mandeville—or Sir John Mandeville, for he describes himself as an English knight in his French or Anglo-Norman text—wrote an account indebted to previous travelers such as Pliny and Odoric of Pordenone. While critical debate over whether his account was pure plagiarism or embroidered from fact has surrounded his text since the late sixteenth century, Mandeville's *Travels* exercised a huge influence over both medieval and early modern travelers. Part compilation of current knowledge and part description of places most Europeans would never visit, the three-hundred-odd extant manuscripts of the *Travels* provide us with a window into the way Europeans conceived of themselves and others.

Much like Odoric and Marco Polo, Mandeville finds marvelous people-animal hybrids in the East, in addition to the usual assortment of cynocephali, sciopods (one-legged men), pygmies, and mythical animals. He even repeats Odoric's claim that in Cathay there are trees that bring forth melons with lambs; the illuminator of BnF fr. 2810 illustrated this marvel with a drawing (fig. 5.4) that could have been used equally well in Odoric's account, which precedes Mandeville's in the compilation.

Tellingly, Mandeville makes an explicit connection between travel to exotic lands and race, thus connecting the voyage to/through the East and its monstrous races with the notion of "race," here seen as physical characteristics linked with moral inferiority and shared within a group of people. Mandeville explains the Great Khan's name by linking it etymologically to Ham, Noah's cursed son. Retelling the biblical story of Noah's nakedness, Mandeville then locates Ham in Africa, attributing Asia to Shem and Europe to Japheth. He claims that most of the evils and deformations of mankind can be found in the lands ruled by Ham's son Cush, including the Tower of Babel. Mandeville writes that

> many devils came in the likeness of men and lay with the women of his race and begat on them giants and other monsters of horrible shape—some without heads, some with dog's heads, and many other misshapen and disfigured men.[29]

The pagan kings of India and the East are descended from Ham, and so the Great Khan took his name from Ham. Mandeville also notes,

> And of Shem, so they say, come the Saracens; and of Japhet the people of Israel and we who live in Europe. This is the opinion of the Saracens and the Samaritans; thus they made me believe until I got to India; when I got there, I well know it was otherwise. Nevertheless it is true that the people of Tartary and all those who live in Greater Asia come from the race of Ham.[30]

Mandeville's geographic confusion, first locating Ham in Africa and then attributing to him large parts of the East, comes from his main reason for classifying the world's races: he wishes to separate the world into Christians (and Jews), Muslims, and all the rest, but he makes this division genealogically. Ham's descendants are part demon, and thus not fully human, resulting in the monstrous races but also in the peoples of Africa and (as he later "realizes") Tartary and Greater Asia. A large section of the world thus has a precarious claim to humanity.

Early Modern Encounters with the Monstrous

The debate about the humanness of unusual peoples did not stop suddenly at the end of what we term the Middle Ages. It continued to appear in Renaissance maps and travel accounts. While medieval mapmakers located the monstrous races in the unexplored areas of the known world, early modern mapmakers relocated these races to the New World, superimposing the physical and metaphorical senses of monstrous margins onto the newly discovered hemisphere.

Juan de la Cosa, an explorer and cartographer who sailed with Christopher Columbus, unknowingly created the oldest extant map of the New World around the year 1500. Still under the impression that they reached Asia, Cosa continues to envision the world in typical medieval fashion, putting two of the monstrous races, the blemmye and the cynocephali, at the very edges of the East, beyond the lands of the "ydolatras" or idol worshippers and the Amazons and not far from the troglodytes, separated from the rest of mankind by a vast river. These monstrous peoples are at the eastern edge of the flat Earth that Cosa depicts; there is no sense that the land wraps around or that there is continuity between Far East and Far West. He has clearly marked, however, the island of the cannibals on the western edge of the map off the coast of Brazil.[31] Since Cosa believed he had reached Asia, the Brazilian cannibals join up spatially with the Far Eastern blemmye and cynocephali, even though they appear on opposite edges of the map.

A few years later in 1513, in the first example of an explicitly New World map, the Ottoman admiral and cartographer Piri Reis shows dog-headed people and blemmye in South America. According to the story written in Turkish on the map, Piri Reis worked from a map obtained from a prisoner who had sailed with Columbus to the Americas on three voyages.[32] His map depicts three dog-men and a blemmye. Like the dog-headed people in Odoric's medieval account, these dog-men appear to possess some degree of culture, often linked to the ability to reason. The couple at the upper left seem to be dancing, while the canine homunculus at the bottom right gestures like a courtier to the blemmye ruler. These animal-man hybrids are located predictably at the very edges of the map, at the extremes of the New World, as if to say that while everyone knows that the monstrous races are not located in India (an area well explored by 1513), they must be found in this new, uncharted land. The Turkish writing on the map does not mention the depicted monstrous races, but the inscription describes the people of the region as animal-like:

it is reported thus, that a Genoese infidel, his name was Colombo . . . discovered these places. . . . not knowing the language of these people, [the Genoese] traded by signs, and after this trip the Bey of Spain sent priests and barley, taught the natives how to sow and reap and converted them to his own religion. They had no religion of any sort. They walked naked and lay there like animals. Now these regions have been opened to all and have become famous.[33]

On this map, the civilizing mission of European explorers connects the indigenous peoples of the Americas with the medieval monstrous races. First, these races occupy the geographical place of the indigenous in the New World. Then, the inscription indicates that the indigenous peoples were animals without culture before the Spanish bestowed on them religion, crop cultivation, and clothing—all markers of the ability to reason.

Renaissance explorers also inherited the notion expounded by Hugh of Saint-Victor that God's grace was moving from East to West. This led some New World explorers to see indigenous Americans as innocents who would eventually be converted, unlike the already corrupted Easterners of India and China. Sixteenth-century French explorer Jacques Cartier recycles the idea of God's salvation moving from East to West in the account of his travels to Canada in the 1530s and 1540s:

> For our first most holy faith was sown and planted in the Holy Land, which is in Asia to the east of our Europe, and afterwards by succession of time it has been carried and proclaimed to us, and at length to the west of our Europe, just like the sun, carrying its light and its heat from east to west, as already set forth.[34]

For Cartier, the village of Hochelaga becomes a prelapsarian earthly paradise, where innocent villagers live a naive but pure existence. The residents are said not to value worldly goods because of their nomadic existence. In the end Hochelaga disappoints Cartier, and he turns his attention to a land described to him by a local chief. This mythical land, called Saguenay, is remote and made in the image of the West. Cartier reports that the chief "let us know that these men are dressed like us and that there are many towns and a large population and good folks, and that they have much gold and copper," and later, "there are white men there as in France and they are outfitted in wool clothing." Cartier's informant also attests to other marvelous races, including a people who "do not eat or have an anus at all and they digest nothing excepting water expelled through the penis. Furthermore it is told that there are pygmies and other lands where the people have only one leg. And other marvels that would take a long time to tell about." Because these are precisely the sorts of places and peoples that the French expect to find in unexplored lands, Cartier insists on capturing his informant to bring him back to France to tell the king firsthand of all that he has seen in his travels. According to a Portuguese visitor to the French court, the elderly chief informs the king of France that he has also seen men who can fly.[35]

Pierre Desceliers, cartographer for Cartier's Canadian voyages, exemplifies the tendency of early modern explorers to apply the ancient and medieval descriptions of monstrous races to New World inhabitants. In his portolan chart of 1546, Desceliers draws a series of mounds near the land of Florida that recall the troglodyte caves of medieval maps.[36] In South America, he notes the lands of giants and of cannibals. In his 1550 map of the world (detail, fig. 5.5), produced following Cartier's second voyage to Canada, he places the pygmies in North America and pictures them shooting cranes, just as described by Pliny and his medieval intellectual descendants. Unicorns also grace the Canadian landscape, pointing to Canada as a land that could embody both the real and the mythical at the same time.

In Cartier's 1541 commission for a third voyage, the people that he has previously encountered are described as "savage peoples living without knowledge of God and without the use of reason," but he also found "peoples of those countries well formed of body and limb and well endowed in mind and understanding."[37] This assessment is found verbatim in another royal commission of 1540, which establishes colonies among the peoples "well formed of body and limb and well endowed in mind and understanding."[38] Following the medieval debate about what constitutes humanness, Cartier describes the inhabitants of Canada as people living like animals, but with a rational soul, giving the French both a right and an obligation to convert these people and move them from animal to human status. The map of Hochelaga in figure 5.6 modifies the basic pattern of the medieval T-O map, making Hochelaga a circular microcosm of the world. At the bottom of the map, the judging angel is replaced by Cartier himself, a telling representation of how Cartier viewed his mission to the New World. He stands at the center, between the people of Hochelaga and the French. Like the angel in Hugh of Saint-Victor's verbal map of the world, it is Cartier who will decide which of these New World "innocents" will be afforded entry to paradise.

Figure 5.5. Detail of Desceliers's 1550 map of Cartier's second voyage to Canada, showing pygmies and unicorns in the New World. BL. Add. MS

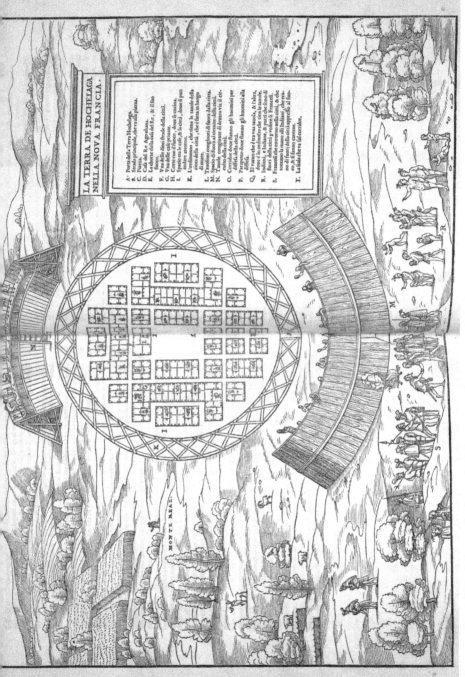

Figure 5.6. Cartier's Hochelaga in the shape of a T-O map. Desceliers, *Mariner's Guide.*

The result of connecting New World inhabitants with the medieval monstrous races, whether used to justify conversion or oppression, was devastating. In his 1547 treatise justifying war against the New World Indians, Juan Ginés de Sepúlveda invokes the idea that the Indians are less than fully human. He addresses a fictional German interlocutor, the antiwar Leopold, who is "somewhat corrupted by Lutheran errors":

> You can well understand, Leopold, if you know the customs and manners of different peoples, that the Spanish have a perfect right to rule these barbarians of the New World and the adjacent islands, who in prudence, skill, virtues, and humanity are as inferior to the Spanish as children to adults, or women to men, for there exists between the two as great a difference as between savage and cruel races and the most merciful, between the most intemperate and the moderate and temperate and, I might even say, between apes and men.[39]

Sepúlveda separates the Indians into different types, claiming that some have no civilization, writing, or rule and thus have no reason and are candidates for natural slavery. For those whom he views as more advanced, he has the following condemnation:

> And as for the way of life of the inhabitants of New Spain and the province of Mexico, I have already said that these people are considered the most civilized of all, and they themselves take pride in their public institutions, because they have cities created in a rational manner and kings who are not hereditary but elected by popular vote, and among themselves they carry on commercial activities in the manner of civilized peoples. But see how they deceived themselves, and how much I dissent from such an opinion, seeing, on the contrary, in these very institutions a proof of the crudity, the barbarity, and natural Slavery of these people; for having houses and some rational way of life and some sort of commerce is a thing which the necessities of nature itself induce, and only serves to prove that they are not bears or monkeys and are not totally lacking in reason.[40]

Sepúlveda argues that these people are born to natural servitude because they own no land individually, but rather all are subject to their king. Thus both rational and irrational humans become ripe for slavery, a conclusion justified on the basis of cultural differences. Like the medieval philosopher Albertus Magnus, Sepúlveda finds that Westerners can encounter people who might seem to be human in form and may even have some amount of "humanness" but still fall short in some critical aspect and are thus discounted as animals.

Eventually and inevitably, Augustine's ambiguous conclusion that the monstrous races either were men and should be saved or were not men became untenable. Augustine might well suggest that blemmye and sciopods are of questionable humanness based on their physical bodies, but the inhabitants of the Americas resembled very much their conquerors. Apologists for Christian colonialists came to the conclusion that these were in fact men without souls, born from spontaneous generation and not descended from Adam.[41]

Equating some ethnic groups with soulless animals lifted the onus of conversion from the colonists and easily justified oppression and exploitation, a line of thought that unfortunately proved extremely difficult to eradicate. In an eerie replay of the medieval debate on the humanness of pygmies, the BBC reported that organizers of a 2007 music festival in Brazzaville, Republic of the Congo, chose to house a group of pygmy musicians in a tent at the city zoo, while all other performers were provided with hotel rooms. A spokesman from the Congolese Observatory of Human Rights pointed out, "It's clear that it's a situation like we saw in earlier centuries, where people put pygmies in zoos to dance or create a spectacle. They were treated the same as zoo animals and I think that we have a similar situation today."[42]

Renaissance appropriation of the medieval discourse on descriptions of Pliny's monstrous races proved to be not a rupture with the medieval past but rather its extension. Medieval travelers continually relocated the monstrous races to unexplored areas; early modern explorers simply reenvisioned their placement in the newest of unexplored lands. These verbal and pictorial images of new peoples were not entertainment. They continued fundamental medieval questions about what makes a being human and what responsibilities Christians have toward these races. As it became clear that New World peoples did not have dog heads or animal bodies, these previously theoretical debates about humanness were transposed onto real peoples, with dire consequences. While medieval debates about humanness were not systematically and institutionally coupled with oppression, they paved the way for intellectual arguments in favor of New World conquest and subjugation. Contrary to the assertion that Renaissance explorers turned away from medieval paradigms, medieval models were integral to early modern conceptions of race and superiority.

6

Conclusions

Medieval Race and the "Golden Age"

Naming this chapter "Conclusions" is from the outset misleading. Just as Columbus, Cartier, and others brought medieval notions of difference to the New World, setting the stage for justifications of slavery persisting into the nineteenth century, fascination with the place of race in the European Middle Ages has not by any means concluded. In general, it seems that the Middle Ages serve as a space that is sufficiently removed from the present that it can be used to explore concepts of importance in the modern world. The European medieval past has become a *lieu de mémoire* or touchstone, a period to which one continually returns because it has been imbued with symbolic meaning far beyond the evidence we have for what really occurred in Europe between 500 and 1500.

One need only consider the number of movies set in the Middle Ages that come out each year, almost all of them embedding some modern conception of difference (race, class, gender, nation) into the story line.[1] (Not to mention the large number of books, plays, "Renaissance fairs," and the like, all of which form a fascinating field of study.) By way of conclusion, this chapter will look at some reimaginings of the Middle Ages, not in an attempt to touch on all the ways that the medieval period creeps into our own, but rather as case studies indicating that the relationship between the European Middle Ages and modern constructions of race— and, more particularly, race relations—is evolving in ways that make the Middle Ages perennially a preferred setting for exploring race.

Movie Medievalism—Re-representing the Past

Movies and visual media provide something that books generally do not: images. Even with no explicit mention of race, the moviegoer can be struck by the visual difference (or lack of difference) that bodies onscreen exhibit. Movies allow directors to remake the past in ways in which the past has not traditionally been conceived. A movie may address directly questions of racial difference in modern society, as *Black Knight* (USA, Junger, 2001) does, or it may show that such differences are constructed and contingent, that their dramatic effects (war, murder, violence) are less about true difference and more related to cultural perceptions of difference, as in *The Song of Roland* (France, Cassenti, 1978). The ultimate purpose of a subset of films set in the medieval past is to allow the director to make a comment on modern race relations—perhaps in order to idealize the past, but also to effect change in the present. Setting an exploration of race relations in a different time and place gives viewers adequate distance from the very real and pressing problems of race relations today. If a film is made in a style that draws viewers in, making them feel like present observers in a past moment in time, then the cinematic view of the past can substitute for any medieval "reality" that historians may attempt to assert. The power of complicity in cinematic forms can forever change a viewer's notion of the Middle Ages, even if the story presented on the screen has no basis in events or conditions that actually occurred.

Casting minorities on the stage and in film has had a troubled history in the United States. Before the 1960s, American and European canonical theatrical pieces were cast almost entirely with white actors. The Non-Traditional Casting Project (NTCP) was established by stage professionals in 1986 with the express goal of increasing the presence of female, ethnic, and disabled actors onstage, particularly in Shakespearean or period pieces.[2] Fairly quickly, however, the aims of the organization came under a dual-pronged attack, with one group protesting historical inaccuracy and yet another group claiming that nontraditional casting was tantamount to asking minorities to "pass" onstage and that what minorities really needed was more plays written and produced specifically for them.[3] However, color-blind casting practices had the overt visionary goal, according to the head of the NTCP, of producing a color-blind audience. This audience, accepting an onstage world where color difference was unimportant, would return to society taking this newly acquired value with them.[4]

Other directors used casting practices that called attention to racial difference and expectations. In one example, in 1982 a theater company performed a version of *Romeo and Juliet* as a biracial tragic love story in a small Mississippi town. White Capulets versus black Montagues replaced the two warring families of Verona, and the play referred specifically to a racially charged incident that had occurred in the local community.[5] Skin color, evident to the audience, made the Shakespearean play take on a new relevance and was an essential part of the message of the director.

Like stage pieces, most medieval films up to the 1990s had no black characters at all.[6] One of the least convincing results of the white-only rule for medieval courtiers was Rex Harrison playing the chivalrous Saladin in heavy, dark makeup in *King Richard and the Crusaders* (USA, Butler, 1954). Since the 1990s, many more roles have been created for minorities in the medieval film genre. Mirroring some of the casting practices seen onstage, medieval films tend either to develop new roles for minority actors, more akin to a color-blind practice, or to intentionally insert racial issues where they would not be expected, thereby focusing the audience's attention on race and even on contemporary or community-specific manifestations of racism.

The 1991 movie *Robin Hood: Prince of Thieves*, directed by Kevin Reynolds, was conceived and filmed during a high point in American multiculturalism, just prior to the backlash epitomized by Dinesh D'Souza's *Illiberal Education* and the 1994 publication of *The Bell Curve*. From the post–World War II period until the late 1980s, the concept that Americans could benefit from learning about each other's culture and history was a cornerstone of American education policy, affirmative action was supported by the U.S. Supreme Court, and noncanonical works made their way onto required reading lists.

Azeem, the black Moor in *Robin Hood: Prince of Thieves* played by Morgan Freeman, incarnates the goals of multiculturalism, as he brings wisdom and cultural advancement to the relatively superstitious and backward English. In a particularly comic scene, Azeem gives Robin a telescope to see the advancing enemy, and Robin believes that the soldiers he sees through the lens are inside the telescope itself. Azeem remarks that he will never understand how Robin's uneducated countrymen could have taken Jerusalem. Azeem's cultural superiority reflects received notions about the preeminence of the Muslim civilization during the time of the Crusades, and his telescope reminds viewers of the technological advances available to Eastern civilization, including the use of refractive lenses and the astrolabe. Azeem manages to win even the rube Friar Tuck to his side when he saves the life of Little John's wife during childbirth by performing an emergency cesarean. The message to the viewer is that, given a chance, other cultures have much to teach the West, even in the fields of science, technology, and medicine.

But Azeem's wisdom is most apparent in his treatment of women.[7] He contrasts the treatment of women in his culture with the way that Robin brags of sexual conquest, noting that in his culture, women can be worth dying for, as opposed to mere sex objects. The idea that a woman can be worth dying for is one that returns at the end as Robin and Azeem prepare to risk their lives in order to save Marian from the sheriff. Robin's transformation from self-centered hero to compassionate leader is complete when he learns Azeem's most valuable lesson and affirms that he now understands how love of a woman is so noble that it could cause a man to put his own life in peril.

The selection of an enlightened black Moor played into America's quest for integration of its African American population. When a small English girl asks, "Did God paint you?" Azeem responds, "For certain, because Allah loves variety." When Friar Tuck calls Azeem a savage, Robin defends him, saying that he is "Savage—like you and me."

The insertion of a black Moor into the tale could also have been motivated by a certain ambivalence about Arabs (the foreign Other, as opposed to blacks, the internal Other) leading up to the First Persian Gulf War, which took place just months before this film was released. The film opens in the Muslim dungeons of Jerusalem, where sadistic Muslims are torturing Christians before killing them. The black Moor is imprisoned with the Christians, highlighting the distinction between good Muslims and bad Muslims. Interestingly, this color-coding parallels and reverses the pattern in the medieval romance epic, where good Muslims are often described as white and bad ones as black-skinned. Director Reynolds, however, does not allow this facile interpretation of good and bad to continue. He later repeats the prison torture motif in England, with the sheriff of Nottingham's prison and torture room looking remarkably similar to those in Jerusalem. In addition, Robin's father denounces Robin's participation in the Crusades, saying that it is vanity to force other men to convert to your religion. Robin's new medieval England is one that accepts color, gender, and religious difference—decidedly not the Middle Ages the historical record would indicate.

If multicultural optimism pervaded *Robin Hood*, ten years later the mood of race relations had taken a decisively pessimistic turn. *Black Knight*, the 2001 film directed by Gil Junger, finds parallels between medieval class stratification and American race-based economic disparity. Jamal Walker, played by Martin Lawrence, is a lackadaisical worker at a medieval theme park who is pulled into fourteenth-century England by a magical amulet. Thinking he has inadvertently wandered into a competing theme park, Jamal's encounter with what he believes to be excessively realistic medieval re-creation produces humorous and anachronistic responses to the low standard of living in this medieval setting. When Jamal meets the drunken knight-errant Nolte, he recognizes that Nolte lives in even worse abjection than those who inhabit American welfare society. He counsels food stamps and checking into a shelter, and even gives Nolte a few dollars for soap and breath mints. Staples of American existence, from toilet paper and fast food to women's rights, are referenced through their lack of medieval counterpart. One lesson that Jamal learns from his trip to medieval England is that standards of living have improved drastically for all segments of society.

One way in which *Black Knight* can give us new insight into medieval literature comes through Jamal's reaction to being called "Moor" by his medieval nemesis, the king's chancellor. Jamal does not initially take umbrage at the term, and "Moor" serves simply as a word used by the Europeans to describe someone clearly foreign and black who has arrived suddenly at court. But as Jamal's influence in the court begins to be felt, the chancellor employs the same term with increasing disdain in his inflection. Finally, as the term becomes the rough equivalent of derogatory uses of "boy," Jamal remarks that he is starting to like the word "Moor" less and less, leading the chancellor to opine that Jamal doesn't know his place in society.

Like the "boy" of twentieth-century American society, "Moor" may be employed with different intents and have diverse connotations about the attitude of the speaker toward the designee. While neither "Moor" nor "boy" necessarily implies racist attitudes, the use of identifiers to connote inferiority may serve as a useful field of inquiry in medieval texts. When Roland refers to his battlefield foes as "pagan" or "Saracen," is this simply a descriptor of religious difference, or does it carry implied racial or ethnic difference? When Nicolette's stepfather tells her that she cannot be involved with Aucassin because she is a *caitive*, is racial or ethnic taint implied, since Nicolette has long since converted and been baptized?

Black Knight cloaks a militant message in its humorous treatment of class difference. From the outset the role of the individual in improving society is contrasted with the impulse toward self-gratification. When Jamal learns that the run-down theme park where he works, Medieval World, will soon be competing with the brand-new Castle World, he suggests to the owner that she sell her operation, take the money, and retire to an easy existence in Florida. The owner, an African American woman, is disappointed by Jamal's reaction, noting that she has provided quality jobs for the community for twenty-seven years. Jamal counsels the owner to help herself and forget about the community, advice he plans to take himself; he later shows his coworker an application to work at the new Castle World and states that he plans to apply before anyone else has a chance, in order to assure a future for himself.

The theme of personal success as opposed to community involvement resurfaces in the medieval world as Jamal finds himself in the midst of a peasants' revolt. The king has overthrown the rightful ruler, a queen who has grassroots support largely composed of the (more) dispossessed of medieval society. Jamal begins by telling himself that this is "not my fight, not my battle." When he turns to help the embattled knight Nolte, he makes a friend who in turn protects him. Jamal goes on to embrace the importance of teamwork, comparing his relationship with Nolte to that of Shaquille O'Neal and Kobe Bryant. When the two return to a camp devastated by the evil king and find a group of peasants who have lost their will to battle the ruler, Jamal turns into the ultimate civil rights leader. He employs the rhetoric of modern-day race relations, turning it into a militant cry for civil rights for all times and places. In particular, he echoes and invokes Rodney King, the African American whose mistreatment at the hands of white police officers provoked race riots in Los Angeles in 1992,[8] using the famous "Why can't we all get along?"

Making a multilayered reference to John F. Kennedy, Jamal remarks, "You, King Leo, are no King Arthur," evoking both the debate in which vice-presidential hopeful Lloyd Bentsen denied Dan Quayle's implication that he was a new JFK and the popular description of the Kennedy White House as Camelot. He then reinforces the reference by proclaiming, "Ask not what your fiefdom can do for you." By linking Kennedy's famous call to civic involvement with the Rodney King scandal, Jamal makes it clear that there are times when one cannot look the other way and think of one's own best interests while an entire community suffers. Rodney King may have wished for a peaceful society, but the riots resulting from his abuse at the hands of white police officers appear to be justified by Jamal's call for communal insurgence.

The relevance of this speech directed at medieval peasantry to current problems is underlined as the director has Martin Lawrence speak toward a spot just to the right or left of the lens, making the moviegoer feel like a member of the medieval audience without disrupting the reality effect by having Lawrence look directly at the camera and break the fourth wall. Earlier in the film Jamal laughs at the concept of civic action when he jokingly calls out "Power to the people!" during a beheading that he thinks is staged. He refuses time and again to fulfill the destiny of the medallion that drew him into the Middle Ages. Yet by the end of the film he comes to realize that the owner of Medieval World was correct when she told him that he needed to think of someone other than himself for once. When he returns to his own society, his coworker encourages him to sue Medieval World for having fallen in the moat. Jamal, thinking of the Medieval World community rather than his own profit, asserts that there is no honor in such a course of action and that instead of seeing himself as a victim, he will lead the fight to improve Medieval World, beat the upstart Castle World, and restore the queen, his boss, to her rightful throne.

Although the films *Robin Hood: Prince of Thieves* and *Black Knight* both allow directors to comment on the state of race relations in contemporary America, Reynolds and Junger take slightly different positions. While *Robin Hood* allows for the inclusion of marginal elements of society, namely women and minorities, the power structures of Reynolds's medieval world remain male and white. *Black Knight* encourages a much more radical notion of how to create an equal society, encouraging violent overthrow of oppressive structures and the empowerment of a black female as a leader. *Robin Hood* uses the historically accurate information that Islamic culture was more advanced than that of the West. *Black Knight* insists that the past was a time of ignorance and discomfort and that even the least privileged members of the modern world enjoy better conditions. Jamal shows no nostalgia for the past, and the medieval period serves as a backdrop for him to learn that the only way to end oppression is to fight those who take advantage of the underclass, even if that fight seems impossible to win. Perhaps the largest difference in the treatment of race in the two films appears in the treatment of their "black knights." In *Robin Hood*, Azeem garners support through quietly but confidently illustrating the superiority of his culture. In *Black Knight*,

Jamal must "pass" in order to gain acceptance. He must become the black knight of myth to inspire respect, capitalizing on superstition rather than reason.

While both *Robin Hood* and *Black Knight* feature black actors in films set in the Middle Ages, neither film depicts a rosy picture for interracial couples. Despite the white king's daughter's interest in Jamal, he remains intrigued by the "Nubian" princess, and Azeem's only connection with the bodies of the white women of England is through the medical emergency of the cesarean he performs. On the contrary, miscegenation was common in medieval courtly literature, as intermarriages occurred between such notable characters as Aucassin and Nicolette, Floris and Blanchefleur, Parzival's father and his first wife, and William of Orange and the Saracen princess Orable, among many others. Medieval attitudes toward race appear at times more tolerant than our own, as in the intermarriage in important families, and at other times remarkably stereotypical and essentialized, as seen in the idea that somehow the Saracen heritage of characters like Nicolette and Orable will continue to resurface even after conversion or, in Nicolette's case, without any prior knowledge of the Saracen culture.

"La geste que Turoldus declinet"

In contrast to cinematic representations of the Middle Ages that show a society tolerant of racial difference, at least one twentieth-century director sought to "correct" medieval racism with his own view of acceptance. When French director Frank Cassenti chose to make a film he titled *La Chanson de Roland* during the 1970s, he eschewed any attempt at faithfully recording history. When asked, Cassenti admitted that he was drawn to the Middle Ages because as a key period far removed from our own, the setting allows us to understand our present.[9] Cassenti, as both director and screenwriter, aimed for a "subjective reconstruction of History that resonates with our present."[10] What we find in Cassenti's *Chanson de Roland* is a personal exploration of what it means to be an author and, more important, what the role of an author is in righting societal wrongs. Charlemagne's crusade into Spain becomes Cassenti's own crusade against racism and injustice in 1970s French society. By first examining Cassenti's conception and construction of the author, we will then be in a position to understand how he arrives at the point where he can claim that the film is a remedy for the racism found in the medieval epic.[11]

The medieval epic known as the *Song of Roland* was never concerned with faithfully recording history. Scholars date the song to about 1100, but the story ostensibly tells of Charlemagne's crusades in Spain, which took place in the late eighth century. One of the greatest conquerors in history, Charlemagne forayed into Spain to reclaim land from Muslims who had come earlier in the century, and in the process he suffered one of his few defeats. He took Pamplona, but his siege of Saragossa failed. He left Spain without any real victory. On his way through the pass back into France, Charlemagne was attacked by other Christians, very likely Basques who had earlier submitted to Charlemagne's father Pepin, and lost some of his men.

From this small amount of historical information, stories were told and retold, changing and expanding on this moment in history. By 1100 the Oxford version of the *Song of Roland* presents us with a tale of treason, intrigue, pride, and punishment. Recast in moralistic terms and cloaked in nascent nationalism, the epic has Charlemagne conquer virtually all of Spain. The only Muslim victory in the campaign—the slaughter of Charlemagne's rear guard, including his nephew Roland—occurs as a result of trickery and the treason of a fellow Christian. The Christian-on-Christian violence of the historical Basque attack on the rear guard becomes a good-versus-evil, Christian-against-Muslim struggle of literally epic proportions. Charlemagne emerges from the conflict in control of all of Spain and as protector of Christian truth. Deforming the past served Christian French society of 1100 well: the *Song of Roland* was used to encourage Christians to take up Urban II's 1095 call to crusade in the Holy Land.

In 1978 Frank Cassenti stepped into the long line of retellers of the *Chanson de Roland*, offering his own cinematic revisioning of France's past while reflecting his society's need to understand its collective history, particularly its tumultuous history of Christian-Muslim conflict. A modern-day Turoldus,[12] Cassenti adapts this thousand-year-old story as a complex web of historical events taking place in the eighth, twelfth, and thirteenth centuries but with clear relevance for twentieth-century France.

Cassenti's film retells Roland's story within a frame tale involving thirteenth-century pilgrims en route to Compostela. The narrative structure of the film is layered, as the twentieth-century audience watches the story of a thirteenth-century pilgrimage where the pilgrims entertain themselves and their hosts by acting out an eleventh-century epic that recounts a purported episode from the eighth-century life of Charlemagne. The pilgrim party has some semiprofessional actors and a jongleur, named Turolde, who tells Roland's story when the pilgrims stop their trek each evening. As the pilgrims wend their way across France on the route to the shrine of Saint James, they perform and dine at the home of a minor nobleman, where the topic of conversation is a peasants' revolt in a neighboring county. The next day, the pilgrims encounter a group of fleeing peasants, who travel alongside the pilgrims for several days. As the pilgrims share their food with the peasants and hear about the atrocities that have been committed, they are clearly moved by the hardships the peasants have faced. When the two groups part ways, the pilgrims' spiritual leader urges the peasants to make their own journey to Compostela. The peasants refuse, and upon departing they quickly perish at the hands of a much better armed group of highborn horsemen seeking revenge. Oblivious to the plight of the peasants, the main group of pilgrims continues on. The actor who plays Roland and two of his companions head north to join another peasant revolt in Flanders.

One of the most striking changes that Cassenti makes to the epic is his refiguring of the Ganelon-Roland conflict. In the Oxford *Roland*, the literary version most commonly read and studied, Ganelon is the archetypical traitor, while Roland figures as an almost Christlike hero whose martyred body is lifted directly from the battlefield to heaven by an angel. In Cassenti's version, Roland's excessive pride and predilection for violent conflict are figured more darkly, giving Ganelon a moral upper hand as he makes his plea for peace with the Muslim armies. In the opening scene, two Muslim horsemen, apparently messengers, approach the Christian army, which stands watching on a hill. No threat can be construed from their approach or demeanor, particularly as they are vastly outnumbered and carry no visible weaponry. Roland gestures to the archers standing beside him, and one of them fatally shoots one of the messengers. The other messenger cries out in Arabic, while the archbishop Turpin, speaking to the camera in a voice that cannot be heard by those around him, tells the remaining "pagan" to go and tell his king that God is helping the Christians and that Charlemagne will prevail. Charlemagne, expressionless, watches the drama unfold in front of him. Roland, then, from the first scene is cast as a maverick who unilaterally makes significant policy decisions, turning what could have been a moment of reconciliation or détente into heightened conflict. Cassenti makes Roland's ambiguous nature evident by shooting Roland with sharply contrasting shadows falling across his face for the entire scene in which he encourages Charlemagne to continue his fight against the Muslims.

Cassenti sets the thirteenth-century plot in parallel with the epic plot, as during the court feast the pilgrims hear about local peasant uprisings. Discussion of this "treasonous" behavior on the part of the peasantry creates tension between those who sympathize with the hungry underclasses and those who declare social roles immutable and sacred. To release the tension, the pilgrims are called on to perform a *geste*, and they pick up where they left off in the *Chanson de Roland* story: the moment of Ganelon's treason. As Thierry, the pilgrim who plays Ganelon, plays the scene, his dislike for Roland is entirely motived by his dislike of Roland's pride and warmongering, which creates a sympathetic connection with modern audiences. The transition back from the epic plot to the pilgrimage plot occurs when Ganelon, upon convincing Charlemagne that there will be no trouble and that Roland should lead the rear guard, collapses against a wall. As Ganelon falls, there is a cut from a distant shot showing all the players to a close-up of Ganelon. At the moment of the fall and the cut, we find ourselves abruptly back in the present of story time, where Thierry has literally collapsed in playing the role of Ganelon. Klaus, who plays Roland, rushes to Thierry's side and explains to onlookers that "he could never play the moment of Ganelon's treason." This inability to betray, even in the interest of peace, further heightens the audience's perception of Ganelon as heroic traitor. His treason tears him apart, but since it is done for the right reasons, the audience is led to understand his motivation and forgive him.

In choosing the *Chanson de Roland* as the subject for a film, Frank Cassenti was faced with the daunting task of putting on celluloid a story that not only was known to every French citizen but, as France's first recognized literary work, had come to define the very historical notion of Frenchness for many. The *Chanson de Roland* has been a staple of the French educational system since Joseph Bédier's 1922 edition.

Cassenti's *Roland* came to fruition a decade after the last of the great Hollywood historical epics, which reached their peak in the 1950s and 1960s. As he struggled to find a suitable vehicle for France's founding epic, Cassenti did not have the luxury of emulating the high-budget Hollywood films. French cinema of the 1970s was largely in a state of crisis, and elaborate sets with casts of thousands were not an option for this relative newcomer. The crisis of French cinema finds its way into the film, according to Cassenti.[13] Cassenti turned in another direction, not seeking to make an epic film, but rather setting out to understand the epic in order to film it. While the *Chanson de Roland* had been part of the national intellectual fabric for fifty years, it had recently returned to center stage as the topic of heated academic debate because of Paul Zumthor's *Essai de poétique médiévale*, published just a few years before Cassenti began work on his film. Zumthor's notion of *mouvance*, that a medieval text existed not as a single unified monument but rather as a series of ever-changing performances and differing manuscripts, transformed the way that authorship and meaning were attributed to medieval works.

Cassenti tells little of the story of Roland, relying on common knowledge of the epic; he focuses instead on the mass creation of a legend. He begins the film with a short scrolling narrative that reads:

> In 778 Charlemagne's rear guard was massacred by Basque looters in the pass of Ronceval. Of these facts, memory has conserved only the legend of the storytellers who sang of Roland and Olivier's prowess in order to make the people forget their great misery. Because the imaginary and the fantastic were a part of the real, pilgrims en route to Saint James of Compostela throughout the twelfth century identified with the heroes of the past in their martyrdom, forgetting for a time the real causes of their suffering. Of history, we retain only its legends.

As an exemplar of the notion that only legends remain of history, within the film the parchment pages that the literate troubadour has so carefully inked with the pilgrims' story are dramatically destroyed during an attack on the group. We know, of course, that the story will eventually make its way to the page, but not this time and not with the story of these same thirteenth-century pilgrims. In keeping with the vagaries of *mouvance*, this particular version of the story will not reach the present day, though its basic elements will.

Creating an Ideology and History in 1970s France

The 1970s marked a turbulent period for Muslims in France. Following World War II, many of the Algerians who had fought on the side of the

Allies expected to become full-fledged members of the French nation. They had understood that if they fought for France, then they would lose their status as the colonized underclass and become citizens. While the French government made some concessions toward Algerian aspirations, full equality was not granted. At the same time, the French government actively encouraged immigration, particularly from North Africa, in part to alleviate the devastation of the French workforce in the two world wars. The massive wave of immigration led to friction and misunderstanding between "old" and "new" French citizens. Meanwhile the push for decolonization and France's initial resistance to granting Algeria its independence eventually resulted in armed conflict. Though the Algerian War officially ended in 1963, Algerians and other North Africans encountered a backlash of sentiment in France for at least a decade. Exacerbated by the economic crisis of the early 1970s, anti-immigrant feeling culminated in 1974 in an official end to labor immigration in France.

In good post–New Wave fashion, Frank Cassenti approached the *Chanson de Roland* not as a literary adaptation but rather as an opportunity to film his own history and to rewrite medieval history to make it relevant. Just as the scribe in the film tells the story of his contemporaries, Cassenti tells the story of his generation. Film critics seemed to sense the political leaning of the film, but they almost universally saw it as a response to the defeat that year of the French Communist Party in the general elections.[14] Cassenti denied this, noting that he had begun the film years before. In an interview, Cassenti stated that he was motivated to make the film in order to address the racism of the medieval version of the *Chanson de Roland*.[15]

Born into a French-Jewish family in Morocco, Cassenti moved to Algeria as an adolescent. When he studied the *Chanson de Roland* in school, he felt the racist dimension of the text and made a connection between "fascist" Roland's imperialistic war and the wars of colonization.[16] Cassenti said no more about racism, but the film treats the Christian-Muslim conflict in a wholly different manner than the medieval epic. The majority of the film plot has a notable absence of Muslims. After the film begins with two lone Muslim horsemen coming to deliver a message to Charlemagne, Muslims are present only at the final battle. The dishonorable attack that Roland instigates on the messengers shows that the source of the conflict is in fact Roland, justifying the massacre that occurs later in the film. Just as the unarmed messenger is shot by Roland's archers, Roland does not die from blowing the horn, as he does in the epic, but rather from a rain of arrows whose parallelism amounts to poetic justice.

Cassenti's work is marked by the pervasive influence of Frantz Fanon, a compatriot whose writings could not have been unknown to the Algerian filmmaker. Following the publication of *Les damnés de la terre* (*The Wretched of the Earth*) in 1961, Fanon was inextricably linked to the notion that change, a break with the past, could be effected only through violence and revolution:

> For the last can be the first only after a murderous and decisive confrontation between the two protagonists. This determination to have the last move up to the front, to have them clamber up (too quickly, say some) the famous echelons of an organized society, can only succeed by resorting to every means, including, of course, violence.[17]

Furthermore, for Fanon, this change could come about only through a revolution led by the rural underclasses, the peasantry, which "has nothing to lose and everything to gain. The underprivileged and starving peasant is the exploited who soon discovers that only violence pays."[18]

Cassenti's *Chanson de Roland* ahistorically creates this same conflict within the confines of thirteenth-century France. True change in the miserable conditions of the medieval underclass, cinematically marked by the filthy and colorless world the peasants inhabit, can take place only through a rejection of what Cassenti terms the fascist legends of the past, embodied in the character of Roland. The dinner discussion between the players and their aristocratic hosts refers to the peasant uprisings and the problem of the peasantry not knowing "their place." Like Fanon, who dwells long on the shortcomings of religion in avoiding necessary violence, Thierry accuses organized religion in the exploitation of the underclasses. Cassenti claims to be challenging the monolithic history of the past, refiguring Roland as a fascist nationalist. Klaus, realizing this, chooses a different path.[19] Klaus joins the peasant revolution and will die, but through his sacrifice and that of his fellow peasants, a history more meaningful than legend will be forged. While the underclass plays a privileged role in Cassenti's film, the unintended communist link with the recent defeat of the PCF does not replace Cassenti's own view that the film was intended to combat the fascism and racism that he found inherent in contemporary French policies toward Muslims. The violence of the underclass in the film is generalizable, referring to the right of any oppressed group to take arms to bring about permanent change.

Klaus's ultimate sacrifice to free the European peasantry ranges far from the medieval oral poems that told of Roland's death at the hands of the Christian Basques in the service of Charlemagne. Cassenti's recasting of the epic inverts exactly what "Turoldus" did when he changed the historical Basque attack on the rear guard to a story of Muslim-on-Christian violence. Cassenti returns the conflict to one of Christian on Christian, class on class, erasing what he perceived to be the racism of the medieval epic. The virtual absence of Muslims in the story points out that real Muslims had very little to do with Europe's crusading ethos. In retelling the *Chanson de Roland*, Cassenti reminds the viewer of the uncomfortable truth: crusades to Spain and the Holy Land had much more to do with internal Western social crisis and conflict than with a desire to see the establishment of truth and justice.

Cassenti, Junger, Reynolds, and other manufacturers of modern medievalism show us the ever-present fascination with the Middle Ages and its capacity for serving as a repository of our own societal concerns. Race is inextricable from our construction of the European medieval period because of the importance race has in our culture today, for which the Middle Ages is a never-ending point of return as place of origin. The beginning and the end turn in upon themselves—the present was and still is understood through the past—so medieval ideas of difference form those of our present, and our present notions refashion our understanding of medieval ones.

Notes

Introduction

1. Book-length studies include Trachtenberg, *The Devil and the Jews*; Chazan, *Medieval Stereotypes and Modern Antisemitism*; Bale, *The Jew in the Medieval Book*; Kessler and Nirenberg, *Judaism and Christian Art*; Hourihane, *Pontius Pilate, Anti-Semitism, and the Passion in Medieval Art*; and Rubin, *Gentile Tales*. Jeffrey Jerome Cohen treats anti-Semitism in several of his works, but also in terms of race in *Hybridity, Identity, and Monstrosity in Medieval Britain*. Geraldine Heng published the two-part article "The Invention of Race in the European Middle Ages" in 2011, and David Nirenberg's book *Anti-Judaism* came out in 2013. These are just some of the many studies that treat medieval anti-Semitism. A few of these, notably Heng's, also briefly treat color prejudice. David Goldenberg's article "Racism, Color Symbolism, and Color Prejudice" makes an eloquent and historicized rationale for the important and unique role color plays in racism.

2. Ramey, *Christian, Saracen and Genre in Medieval French Literature*.

3. This term is used to indicate that the medieval period was not pre-racial, as in color-blind, but in the process of forming a racially based social system.

4. Studies like Frank Snowden's *Before Color Prejudice* on ancient Greece and Rome and David Goldenberg's *The Curse of Ham* on early Jewish writing make it their goal to prove that racial consciousness did indeed begin at some period, but not in the period that they study.

Chapter 1. Remaking the Middle Ages

1. Emery and Morowitz, *Consuming the Past*, 1.

2. See for example the essays by Nichols, Graham, Hult, Peck, Nykrog, and Boureau in Bloch and Nichols, *Medievalism and the Modernist Temper*.

Almost every essay in this insightful volume on the history of medieval studies touches on the nationalistic aspect of the writings of the nineteenth-century "founders" of the Middle Ages.

3. In Irving, *The Alhambra* (1969), vi–vii.

4. For example, Hendrix, "New Vision of America"; LeMenager, "Trading Stories."

5. Bowden, *Washington Irving*, 55.

6. Blumenbach, *Natural Varieties of Mankind*, 264–65, as quoted in Gould, *The Mismeasure of Man*, 412. This ranking system is not unlike the medieval Great Chain of Being; see Lovejoy, *Great Chain*, and an expanded discussion of this concept in chapter 5.

7. Some of these thinkers, including Houston Stewart Chamberlain (1855–1927) and Ernest Renan (1823–1892), are listed by Ivan Hannaford in *Race*, esp. 348–56.

8. The history of race theories shows fascinating movement between categories for various peoples. One excellent source of general information on race history is Banton, *Racial Theories*. Banton sees the first two "phases" of race history as a need to classify and distinguish different sorts of people, then to explain order and superiority of groups of people. The third phase for Banton is based on genetic selection and answers a different set of questions. As Banton explains, the questions and answers change—the answer to the problem "Why is the Negro's skin black?" changed from "Because of a biblical curse" to "Because it has always been black" and then to "Because it confers a selective advantage in certain environments" (7). See Fredrickson's *Racism* for a concise overview of the history of racism. He charts the importance of Enlightenment thought and the later bifurcation into Nazi anti-Semitism and American antiblack currents of racism. As Fredrickson notes, ethnologists saw Semites as Caucasian, so "whiteness" was not sufficient for Nazi rhetorical purposes, hence the rise of the Aryan myth for the specifically political purpose of delineating the German and northern European peoples as the culturally superior branch of humanity, or master race (90).

9. A good article summarizing the historical development of race theory and the problems arising from the history of this idea is Lucius Outlaw's "Toward a Critical Theory of 'Race.'" Outlaw points out the convenient association of black with sin in the Christian context that facilitated the early "career" of race in premodern Europe (62). His article goes on to say that critical theory has gotten caught up in arguments that, while

important, may have overlooked the lived experience of racial groups to-day. The United States, as the inherently racial state of Omi and Winant's *Racial Formation in the United States*, needs a new critical theory of race that can accommodate the lived experience of diverse groups. Outlaw's vision of the "career" of race that stretches from an early Christian association of black with sin to today's racial state manages to show clearly that there is indeed a difference between early notions of race and a racial state without negating the importance of the early history or presence of racial thought.

10. See Bloch and Nichols, *Medievalism and the Modernist Temper*, as well as the more recent work by Burde, "The Song of Roland in Nine-teenth-Century France."

11. See Fischer, *Modernity Disavowed*; Dubois, *A Colony of Citizens*; Dobie, *Trading Places*; Miller, *The French Atlantic Triangle*.

12. Irving, *Astoria*, 152. For more on Irving's view of miscegenation in the American West, see LeMenager, "Trading Stories."

13. Jeffrey Scraba in "'Dear Old Romantic Spain'" reveals the ironic romanticism Irving uses in his novelistic portrayal of this period of Spanish history. Irving's narrator is a Christian monk who makes no bones about his opposition to the Muslim invaders, but the monk is so overtly partisan and extreme that it makes him seem slightly ridiculous. Irving's stance on the Islamic Conquest is anything but clear, but his later, continued romanticizing of the Islamic reign at the Alhambra makes his sympathies for the onetime invaders evident.

14. Irving, *The Alhambra* (1969), 9.

15. Ibid., 164. Most of Spain was settled by Visigoths in the late antique period (fifth century) and then came under Islamic Umayyad rule between 711 and 718. The Christian "Reconquest" of Spain began almost immediately but did not end definitively until 1492.

16. Irving, *The Alhambra* (1832).

17. Irving, *The Alhambra* (1969), 15.

18. Ibid., 16.

19. Ibid., 16–17.

20. Ibid., 156.

21. Ibid., 15.

22. Ibid.

23. For example, in Irving, *The Alhambra* (1851), 59, as the narrator passes through the Alhambra, he imagines the palace peopled and vibrant

as it was when the home to a great court. In one of these romantic apparitions of the past, a "white arm of some mysterious princess" beckons from behind the screen of the serail.

24. See note 9.

25. Irving, *Astoria*, 136.

26. Darley was considered the premier illustrator of his time. Apparently his work met with approval, as he was further commissioned to illustrate Irving's *Sketch Book, Knickerbocker's History*, and *Tales of a Traveller*. At his home in Sunnyside, New York, Irving displayed a series of Darley's sketches including seven from the Alhambra, which prompted Andrew Breen Myers in his introduction to *The Alhambra* (1982) to claim that Irving must have approved and even delighted in Darley's work.

27. I would argue that the illustrator has in fact misread the story. Firstly, the astrologer was to be an old man, which does not appear to be the case with the black Moor. Also, the story says that the astrologer "seized the bridle of the palfrey, smote the earth with his staff, and sank with the Gothic princess through the centre of the barbican." The bridle that the astrologer (with the staff) grabs in the image is not that of the palfrey (the Gothic princess' horse) but that of the king.

28. As historian Pamela Toler points out (private communication), the princess avoids miscegenation with both the white and the black Muslim, indicating perhaps a religious issue. This could also point to a refusal to mix the Semitic with the northern European Gothic. At any rate, it is indeed impossible to imagine what Washington Irving's take on race and miscegenation at this point might have been—complicated, for sure.

29. Irving, *The Alhambra* (1969), 136.

30. See also Scraba, "'Dear Old Romantic Spain,'" 275–95. Scraba suggests that Irving rehabilitates Boabdil, who has gone down in Spanish history as a fully execrable figure, as an ironic reflection on the tension between romanticism and history. I suspect Irving's rehabilitation of Boabdil was more likely linked to Boabdil's purity of race.

31. Ibid., 279–81.

32. The premier medievalist in France in the late nineteenth century, Gaston Paris, gave extraordinary weight to the *Chanson de Roland* as a poem of national unity, culminating in an inaugural lecture he gave to the Collège de France in 1870 titled "La Chanson de Roland et la nationalité française." See Hult, "Gaston Paris and the Invention of Courtly Love," 195. In Bloch and Nichols, *Medievalism and the Modernist Temper*, in addition

to Hult's essay, see those of Nichols and Graham, which treat the conflu-
ence of national identity, nationalism, and medieval studies in France and
Germany.

33. Murphy, *Memory and Modernity*, 22.

34. Viollet-le-Duc, *Dictionnaire raisonné*, "Restoration," vol. 8, 14–34,
translated in Hearn, *Architectural Theory*, 195.

35. John Summerson in "Viollet-le-Duc," 7, calls him the "last great the-
orist in the world of architecture" and one of only two great architectural
theorists ever.

36. M. F. Hearn in *Architectural Theory*, 14, includes Le Corbusier,
Frank Furness, and Frank Lloyd Wright among the many who acknowledge a significant debt to Viollet-le-Duc.

37. Barot, Yung, and Alglave, *Revue des cours littéraires*.

38. The term *translatio studii* (transfer of knowledge) was used by the
medieval West because they considered that God had entrusted them
with the intellectual legacy of the Greeks, passed first to the Roman Empire and then, as that empire waned, to the West.

39. Viollet-le-Duc, *Histoire de l'habitation humaine*, 7.

40. Ibid., translated in *Habitations*, 7.

41. Viollet-le-Duc is making the connection here with "Aryans," a term
that evolved over time to become increasingly charged with meaning. At
first, in the early to middle part of the nineteenth century, it referred to a
linguistic group and would have included Semitic peoples, as per Blumenbach. A few decades later it would refer increasingly to northern Europeans, and then during the Nazi regime to the master race.

42. Viollet-le-Duc, *Habitations*, 12.

43. Ibid., 347.

44. Ibid., 373–74.

45. Ibid., 391.

46. Ibid., 391–92.

47. Barot, Yung, and Alglave, *Revue des cours littéraires*, 151, my translation.

Chapter 2. Medieval Race?

1. While more recent work on medieval race has been done and will be
referenced in this chapter, skin color remains an area often neglected by
medievalists. Earlier work, like James Muldoon's "Race or Culture: Medieval Notions of Difference," in which he says—echoing what classicist

Frank Snowden said of the ancient world—that "racism as we understand the term did not exist and skin color was not a mark of inferiority or of slavery" (79), has not been significantly supplanted. Geraldine Heng had already noted the importance of skin color in *Empire of Magic*, 15, 64, 230, and esp. 340–41nn. Heng's most recent work is clearly moving in the direction of a deeper reading of the ambivalence of the medieval treatment of black persons in cultural production; see "Invention of Race," 285. Lucius Outlaw (not a medievalist) noted somewhat in passing but with conviction the impact that equating black with evil and white with good in the Bible had on early Christian and medieval culture ("Critical Theory," 62). Clarence Glacken in *Traces on the Rhodian Shore* does not use the term "race," but his chapter 6 discussion of medieval European perceptions of difference is a highly useful introduction to the variety of medieval sources that contrast bodily differences in humans.

2. Eliav-Feldon, Isaac, and Ziegler, *Origins*, 7. This rather handy definition is immediately questioned by the book's editors, who note that "race" as a category with any real meaning is under fire by geneticists at this time.

3. Ibid., 10–12, citing Albert Memmi, whose definition I paraphrase. Eliav-Feldon, Isaac, and Ziegler would also allow for a "positive" racism, it would appear, in that a comment such as "Asians are smart" or "Blacks have rhythm" can be seen as racist. I would agree, mainly because such comments often serve to reduce a particular individual's accomplishment to some sort of unfair genetic advantage. Christian Delacampagne, locating racism in the ancient and medieval West, uses a variant of this definition and echoes Anthony Appiah. See Delacampagne, "Racism and the West," 85.

4. Fredrickson, *Racism*. Fredrickson dips briefly into the late medieval period to discuss the persecution of Jews, but he sees religion as the main discourse of racism in the Middle Ages. While Fredrickson is not incorrect in his observations about the importance of the religious aspect of the construction of race, this does not obviate the question of an early importance of skin color and genetic notions to racial constructions.

5. Eliav-Feldon, Isaac, and Ziegler, *Origins*, 200–216.

6. "From the first, therefore, the term focused on natural—what we would now call biological—differences and placed great value on the possession of inherited character traits" (Boulle, "François Bernier," 12).

7. Ibid., 20.

8. A more distinct definition of racism was put forward by historian

George Fredrickson (*Racism,* 6) as something that is espoused by a group who have the power to establish a racial order and that is believed to reflect the laws of nature or of God. This ability to wield power over another individual is a defining characteristic of racism for Fredrickson, which would mean that in 1960s America, an African American would be guilty of ethnocentrism rather than racism if he or she discriminated against a white person.

9. For example, Jews in America across just one generation considered themselves "white" while their parents did not; see Brodkin, *How Jews Became White,* 175.

10. What the word "race" means to each person is clearly different, and the word means something very different to me now than it did when I first began this study almost a decade ago. Looking at what race may have meant in the Middle Ages has necessarily been a long, fascinating, sometimes discouraging, sometimes hopeful, reflection on what it means in the United States today. Presentism seems like an unfruitful concept to me; at least, those who study the past should not always be forced into estranging the past, thinking "us versus them." Some of the most creative thinking about the past sees uncanny resemblances between us and them.

11. This suggestion was made by an audience member at the Medieval Academy of America meeting of 2004 in Seattle when I gave an early version of chapter 3 as a paper titled "Medieval Western Views of Conception and Literary Miscegenation."

12. This uncomfortable relationship between the medieval and the modern has been examined by Kathleen Biddick in *The Shock of Medievalism.*

13. Delacampagne, *L'invention du racisme.* In "Racism and the West" Delacampagne further defends his genealogy of racism and allies himself with Anthony Appiah and other race theorists who see the beginning of racism as "when one makes (alleged) cultural superiority directly and mechanically dependent on (alleged) physiological superiority, that is, when one *derives* the cultural characteristics of a given group from its biological characteristics" (85).

14. Nepaulsingh, "The Continental Fallacy of Race," 143.

15. Akbari, "From Due East to True North," 27.

16. Ibid., 31.

17. For an excellent overview of this question, see Goldenberg, "Racism."

18. Goldenberg, *The Curse of Ham,* 96.

19. See Bartlett, "Illustrating Ethnicity," esp. 134–37; Devisse, *From the*

Early Christian Era to the "Age of Discovery." Bartlett in "The Face of the Barbarian" also discusses the importance of medieval ethnographic interpretations on later English views of other groups, for example the Irish. He traces New World prejudices against the Irish to Anglo-Norman depictions in the twelfth century.

20. K. Campbell, *Literature and Culture in the Black Atlantic*, 36.

21. Robert Bartlett in "Illustrating Ethnicity," 137, sees representations of this black saint as indicating the universal nature of the Christian mission—even blacks could be redeemed. Geraldine Heng writes in "Invention of Race," 285, of the aesthetic pleasure of the black figure of Maurice and also calls for a move to considerations of color.

22. Freedman, *Images of the Medieval Peasant*.

23. See for example Heng, "Invention of Race," 285.

24. Studies including Howard Bloch's *Medieval Misogyny* have shown that in the medieval period praise of "good" examples can in fact indicate a high level of prejudice. For example, in the case of women, the Virgin was often held up as an inimitable model, underscoring the perceived shortcomings of medieval women. See also Blamires, *Woman*, 171–98, and *Case*.

25. Dayan, *The Law Is a White Dog*, 139–40.

26. The debate about the humanness of pygmies will be taken up in detail in chapter 5.

27. Karl Steel's thoughtful book *How to Make a Human* illustrates the difficulty that medieval thinkers had delineating the animal from the human and the intellectual and cultural work that began in the Middle Ages to arrive at the split between the animal and human.

28. The definitive work remains E. P. Evans, *The Criminal Prosecution and Capital Punishment of Animals*. This book details the prosecutions and executions of animals ranging from insects to horses for various crimes against humans.

29. These populations are recorded frequently in travel literature, including the *Travels* of John Mandeville and *Marvels of the East*. See M. Campbell, *The Witness and the Other World*.

30. See Bartholomaeus, *Properties of Things*, chap. 15. Even the nakedness that Odoric of Pordenone notes in his travels causes questions about the humanity of the peoples he encounters, since clothing is one of the hallmarks of humanness, according to Augustine, *City of God* 14.17, and Hugh of Saint-Victor, Didascalicon 1.9, as cited in Friedman, *Monstrous Races*, 255n29.

31. Augustine, *City of God* 16.8.

32. Gratian C.23 q.5 c.13; Friedberg and Richter, *Corpus iuris canonici*, vol. 1, col. 1254.

33. As translated by Tolan in *Petrus Alfonsi*, 117.

34. The relationship between gender and race in the development of this rhetoric deserves further attention. Jacqueline de Weever's *Sheba's Daughters* takes on the issue of race and gender in medieval French epic, but her work, while very useful, leaves aside feminist criticism, and much work on race theory has been done in the interim. The importance of anti-Semitism to the building of this discourse cannot be overstated; for a selected list of works on this topic, see note 1 to the introduction. Locating the nexus of color prejudice, misogyny, and anti-Semitism would be a fascinating and unwieldy topic, perhaps best handled on a micro level, with a particular case or text at a specific time and place.

35. For a comprehensive survey of the scholarship, see Lampert-Weissig, *Medieval Literature and Postcolonial Studies*.

36. Bhabha, "Of Mimicry and Man," 130.

37. Bhabha, *The Location of Culture*, 53–56.

38. See Linda Lomperis's discussion of mimicry in her study of Mandeville, "Medieval Travel Writing and the Question of Race."

39. Most romance epics are dated to the twelfth and thirteenth centuries. Following the thesis I developed in *Christian, Saracen, and Genre in Medieval French Literature*, they illustrate a period of time and a propensity for a genre that would allow for both contact (through crusade) and desire. These particular works have an interesting critical history that exceeds the scope of this work, but in short they have traditionally been read as a separate genre from the more "masculine" epic without a real love interest like the *Chanson de Roland*. The imaginary possibility of intermarriage or hybridity, specific to the political context of conversion politics and the Crusader kingdoms in the twelfth and thirteenth centuries, made this ambiguously optimistic genre hugely popular for a specifically delimited period of time.

40. Balibar, "Sub specie universitatis," 10.

41. Ibid., 11.

42. The Crusader kingdoms were small feudal states established in the twelfth and thirteenth centuries around Jerusalem and elsewhere in the Near East, including Cyprus, and up into the Baltic region. These communities represented territorial gains for Western Europeans and often had

Christians, Jews, Muslims, and/or pagans living relatively harmoniously for brief periods of time. For an excellent overview and great classroom resource available in French and English, see Tate, *The Crusades and the Holy Land.*

43. Lomperis, "Medieval Travel Writing," 148.

44. Ibid., 149.

45. See for example Guzman, "Encyclopedist Vincent." The relevant passage can be found in Vincent, *Speculum quadruplex*, vol. 4, col. 1288.

46. Guzman, "Encyclopedist Vincent," 291.

47. Ibid. In the first, a recalcitrant widow is forced to consummate a marriage with her deceased husband's younger brother (also unwilling) in front of an insistent gathering; Mongols are expected to marry their late brothers' wives. The other custom is polygamy.

48. Ruggles, "Mothers of a Hybrid Dynasty," 69.

49. Lampert, "Race," 419; Appiah, "Race."

50. Lampert, "Race," 394; Appiah, "Race."

51. Lampert-Weissig gives further examples of "how somatic differences typically associated with ideas of race have been linked to representations of religious difference" (*Medieval Literature and Postcolonial Studies*, 73).

52. Lombroso, *Criminal Man.*

53. W. Jordan, "Why Race?," 169.

54. Again, the contention of Biddick in *The Shock of the Medieval*, but the danger and limitations of drawing too neat a line between medieval and Renaissance is also an important point of many recent studies, including Caferro, *Contesting the Renaissance.*

55. Heng, "Invention of Race," 263.

Chapter 3. Biblical Race

1. I am using the term "Saracen" because it (or "pagan") is the vague and inaccurate term that was used at the time. These characters are fictional constructs and not historical Muslims, for whom I use different terminology.

2. Many medieval commentaries and even some of the later stories do not have obvious lines of transmission between Jewish commentators, Christian thinkers, and medieval authors. This lack of documentable cultural borrowing could be seen as problematic: if we cannot know that some of these cultural stories were shared, how can we use them

as examples? While that argument has merit, there are of course many other documented examples of "sharing" of religious and cultural beliefs, including the disputations of fifteenth-century Spain. See, for example, Daniel J. Lasker's *Jewish Philosophical Polemics against Christianity in the Middle Ages* and Hyam Maccoby's *Judaism on Trial: Jewish-Christian Disputations in the Middle Ages.* Everyday contact between cultures in Crusader kingdoms, Spain, Sicily, and around the Mediterranean basin as well as the cities of Europe provided the opportunity for informal exchange of tales and beliefs that will never be traceable or scientifically proven. The existence of such beliefs in one culture is proof enough that such beliefs might well have spread to other contingent cultures, through time and space.

3. "locutaque est Maria et Aaron contra Mosen propter uxorem eius aethiopissam." Latin quotations are from the Vulgate Bible. Both the Vulgate and the Douay-Rheims translation are available online.

4. "nubes quoque recessit quae erat super tabernaculum et ecce Maria apparuit candens lepra quasi nix cumque respexisset eam Aaron et vidisset perfusam lepra."

5. For a thorough history of the controversies surrounding the account, see Karen S. Winslow's "Moses' Cushite Marriage: Torah, Artapanus, and Josephus."

6. Josephus, *Jewish Antiquities*, bk. 2, chap. 2. The story is found in the Loeb edition, 1: 270–75. The histories of Moses and his marriage come from Avigdor Shinan's "Moses and the Ethiopian Woman: Sources of a Story in the *Chronicles of Moses*." Artapanus's history is a fragment cited in other, later sources, namely Clement of Alexandria and Eusebius.

7. Shinan, "Moses and the Ethiopian Woman," 74.

8. Halter, *Zipporah.*

9. Some historians conflate Ethiopians and Cushites during Solomon's reign, while others make a distinction. Many use the terms interchangeably. It is truly beyond the scope of this study to tease out whether the Cushites during this period were "black" or "white," nor is it particularly of interest here. What is important is that some historians and theologians believe(d) it necessary to create elaborate justifications and lineages so that this bride could possibly be "white" or Semitic as opposed to black.

10. Genesis 9:20–25, Douay-Rheims. The Douay-Rheims Bible is a sixteenth-century English translation of the Latin Vulgate, which was the official Catholic Bible in the Middle Ages.

11. Goldenberg, *The Curse of Ham*, 105–6. He locates this in a ninth-century precursor (*Pirqei de-Rabbenu ha-Qadosh*) to Rashi's and Nathan b. Yehiel's eleventh-century commentaries on the Talmud, where the black skin is limited to Ethiopia/Kush and not darker skin in general, which would include Egyptians and others.

12. Burgess and Strijbosch, *The Brendan Legend*, p. 38, line 310.

13. See Devisse, *From the Early Christian Era to the "Age of Discovery."* For further reading on Ethiopians as seen in ancient cultures, see also Gay L. Byron's *Symbolic Blackness and Ethnic Difference in Early Christian Literature*, 37–51.

14. Fellous, *Histoire de la Bible de Moïse Arragel*, 164. The reproduced miniature is in Genesis, folio 33rb.

15. The T-O maps were discussed in chapter 2. For the importance of these medieval maps and their indications of premodern notions of race, see both Akbari and Nepaulsingh.

16. Several scholarly works have been devoted to the stories of Sheba. One of the earliest, dealing with Ethiopian travel and spread of the Kebra Nagast, is O.G.S. Crawford's *Ethiopian Itineraries, Circa 1400–1524* (1958). For an excellent article on the history of the medieval myth of Sheba, see "From Sheba They Come: Medieval Ethiopian Myth, US Newspapers, and a Modern American Narrative," by Wendy Laura Belcher.

17. For the Jewish and Islamic traditions, see Jacob Lassner's *Demonizing the Queen of Sheba*. For the Christian tradition, see de Weever, *Sheba's Daughters*; Clapp, *Sheba*, esp. chap. 3. Clapp's book is an interesting mix of scholarship and personal narrative as he searches for Sheba. Sheba is the subject of a similar hunt in Wood, *In Search of Myths*.

18. Wood, *In Search of Myths*, 149.

19. Josephus, *Jewish Antiquities* (Loeb edition), 3:304–9 on Sheba; 3:316–21 on Solomon's foreign women; "He surpassed all other kings in good fortune, wealth and wisdom, except that as he approached old age he was beguiled by his wives into committing unlawful acts" (3:329).

20. The Kebra Nagast is a central religious text for Ethiopian Christians and Rastafarians. The origins of the text are not without dispute, but it is believed to be at least seven hundred years old. It is likely that oral tales concerning Sheba predate the first known composition of the Kebra Nagast in the mid-fourteenth century.

21. The complete tale can be found in E. A. Wallis Budge's *The Queen of Sheba and Her Only Son Menyelek: The Kebra Nagast*.

22. Clapp, *Sheba*, 60–65.

23. The value of women as gifts between men in some societies is well documented; see Claude Levi-Strauss for pioneering work in *Elementary Structures of Kinship* (1949). Megan Moore's recent work in *Exchanges in Exoticism* on the role of foreign women in medieval Franco-Byzantine cultural exchange indicates that this is a fruitful area for further exploration.

24. My reading is particularly indebted to *The Song of Songs in the Middle Ages* by Ann W. Astell, who notes a shift in the way that the song was interpreted starting in the twelfth century. For more details on the popularity of the song, see her introduction.

25. DeSimone, *Bride and the Bridegroom*.

26. Ibid., chap. 1, v. 5.

27. Origen, *Commentaire*. Origen was quite prolific, and his work was in broad circulation until he was condemned for heresy (after his death) in 543 and again in 553. Much of his work was destroyed following that condemnation, but his work was so influential that he continues to be seen as one of the first theologians of the Church and a Church Father. For a summary of his work and what we know about his life, see Matter, *Voice of My Beloved*, 20–48.

28. Nilus, *Commentaire*.

29. On this change, see Mervyn C. Alleyne's *The Construction and Representation of Race and Ethnicity in the Caribbean and the World*, 50.

30. These are the most commonly used English-language Bibles today. While not a specific goal, I was unable to find a single English translation that used "black and beautiful." The Hebrew versions, both ancient and modern, indicate "black *and* beautiful." Young's Literal Translation renders this: "Dark am I, and comely, daughters of Jerusalem, As tents of Kedar, as curtains of Solomon." The Latin Vulgate has: "nigra sum sed formosa / filiae Hierusalem / sicut tabernacula Cedar / sicut pelles Salomonis."

31. Apponius, *Commentaire*, 57.

32. Ibid., 205–7. Asenath is briefly mentioned in the Bible (Genesis 41:45, 50) as the Egyptian princess who is married to Joseph, though a longer romance tradition surrounds their love story. For further reading, see Kraemer, *When Aseneth Met Joseph*.

33. Apponius, *Commentaire*, 206, my translation.

34. This interpretation goes counter to Jacqueline de Weever's read-

ing in *Sheba's Daughters*. De Weever finds the commentaries to be metaphorical from the very beginning. This difference in interpretation does not diminish her argument that the black heroines must be whitened in medieval French literature in order to be acceptable marriage partners. Indeed, by the time vernacular literature takes root in the eleventh and twelfth centuries, that is very much the case.

35. Leclercq, *Monks and Love*, 8–26.

36. A theological example of this difference would be that Origen's theories allowed for a salvation of the soul alone, whereas Augustine paved the way for the doctrine of Bodily Resurrection.

37. Astell, *Song of Songs*, 1–24. For the role of the feminine in the twelfth century, see Bynum, *Resurrection of the Body*.

38. Astell, *Song of Songs*, 9.

39. The quotation and translation are taken from Sermon 40 in Bernard of Clairvaux's *On the Song of Songs I*. These sermons were likely written and meant to be read as opposed to taken down from actual performances by a scribe. See the introductory essay by Jean Leclerq in *On the Song of Songs II*.

40. Ibid., sermon 28.

41. It is also of note that some of the most important modern studies on the Song of Songs, including Matter, Astell, and Bynum, deal with women and the feminine, but not the question of "race" or blackness at all, though this was clearly a major focus of the medieval commentators.

42. Aristotelianism and Augustinianism were at odds on the question of bodily resurrection, as Caroline Walker Bynum shows in *Resurrection of the Body*, 230. Some thirteenth-century commentaries on the Song of Songs could reflect this tension—potential grounds for further inquiry.

43. Nicholas of Lyra, *Postilla*, 31.

44. Ibid.

45. Ibid., 33.

46. Ibid., 33–35.

47. Ibid., 39.

48. Bloch, *Medieval Misogyny*, 31.

49. Ibid., 90.

50. Ibid., 91.

51. See chapter 2 for a discussion of Colin Dayan's work.

52. This is Jacqueline de Weever's argument in *Sheba's Daughters*.

53. See chapter 2 for discussion of incomplete conversion.

54. Boccaccio, *Concerning Famous Women*, xii.

55. Jeanroy, "Boccace, Christine," 94.

56. C. Jordan, "Boccaccio's In-Famous Women," 26.

57. Pizan, *City of Ladies*, 7.

58. Ferrante, "Public Postures," 226.

59. Pizan, *City of Ladies*, 33.

60. Ibid.

61. Ibid., 105.

62. Ibid., 106.

63. Ibid.

64. de Weever, *Sheba's Daughters*; the importance of the erasure of blackness for Old French heroines is the main argument of the entire book.

65. Here I am using the term as adopted for the medieval period by Kofi Campbell in *Literature and Culture in the Black Atlantic*.

Chapter 4. Medieval Miscegenation and the Literary Imagination

1. Laqueur, *Making Sex*, 30. See also Baldwin, *The Language of Sex*.

2. Laqueur, *Making Sex*, 123–30. In the fourteenth-century French *Miracle de la fille d'un roy* (Paris and Robert, *Miracles*, 7:1–117) a girl is raised as a boy, falls in love with a girl, and after much prayer is transformed into a boy by the Virgin when she/he is about to be literally uncovered for who she/he is. Sexual transformation, like race transformation, could be brought about through prayer and divine intervention.

3. Aristotle, *Generation of Animals*, bk. 3.

4. Cadden, *Meanings of Sex Difference*, 18.

5. Ibid., 21. The twelfth century saw a renewal of ancient learning through several translation projects centered in Toledo. Gerard of Cremona is credited with making available in the West many new sources of Greek philosophy that had been preserved in Arabic, including portions of Aristotle and Galen.

6. For an excellent summary of Isidore's thoughts on sexual reproduction, see Laqueur, *Making Sex*, 55–56.

7. Isidore, *The Medical Writings*, 48.

8. Literally "God's judgment," the *judicium dei* refers to the concept that the outcome of a battle decides which side must have been in the right, since God is on the side of the righteous.

9. For example, in the *Chanson de Roland*, Roland states baldly, "Paien unt tort e chrestïens unt dreit" [pagans are wrong and Christians are right] (line 1015). All citations of the epic in Old French are from the Cortés Vázquez edition of 1994.

10. Studies of monstrous births in medieval thought are abundant, though most such births are not due to miscegenation. Some possibilities for deformed children include the sinful nature of the mother, conception during menstruation, and disturbing thoughts and visual stimulation of the mother during gestation. See Kappler, *Monstres*; Gilbert, "Unnatural Mothers"; Atkinson, *The Oldest Vocation*.

11. Atkinson, *The Oldest Vocation*, 25.

12. "As white as feþer of swayn" (12). All citations of *The King of Tars* are from the English Poetry Full-Text Database. This romance is found in three manuscripts: National Library of Scotland Advocates' MS 19.2.1 (Auchinleck manuscript), Bodleian 3938 (Vernon manuscript), and British Library Add. MS 22283. Translations into English are mine with advice from my colleague John Plummer (all mistakes mine, of course).

13. "Wel loþe was a cristenman, / To wedde an he þen woman, / Þat leued on fals lawe; / Als loþ was þat soudan, / To wed a cristen woman, / As y finde in mi sawe" (406–11).

14. "& when þe child was y-bore, / Wel sori wimen were þer fore, / For lim no hadde it non; / Bot as a rond of flesche y-schore / In chaumber it lay hem before, / Wiþ outen blod & bon. / For sorwe þe leuedi wald dye, / For it hadde noiþer nose no eye, / Bot lay ded as þe ston" (574–82).

15. Gilbert, "Unnatural Mothers," 335.

16. "'O, dame,' he sayd bi forn, / 'Oyain mi godes þou art forsworn, / Wiþ riyt resoun y preue: / Þe childe, þat is here of þe born, / Boþe lim liþ it is for-lorn, / Alle þurch þi fals bileue'" (586–91).

17. "Leue sir, lat be þat þouyt; / Þe child, was yeten bitven ous to" (600–601).

18. "Feirer child miyt non be bore; / It no hadde neuer a lime forlore, / Wele schapen it was wiþ alle" (775–77).

19. "Ya, sir, bi seyn Martin, / Yif þe halvendel wer þin, / Wel glad miyt þou be" (802–4).

20. "Bot þou were cristned so it is, / Þou no hast no part þeron, / y-wis Noiþer of þe child ne of me / ' . . . & yif þou were a cristen man, / Boþe were þine,' sche seyd þan, / 'Þi childe & eke þi wiue'" (808–19).

21. Laqueur, *Making Sex*, 123–30.

22. *The King of Tars*, 12.

23. John Block Friedman notes in *Monstrous Races*, 67, that the Muslim is often portrayed as a dog, both in image and word, in the Middle Ages.

24. *The King of Tars*, 448.

25. "His hide, þat blac & loþely ws, / Al white bicom þurch godes gras / & clere wiþ outen blame" (922–24).

26. Jane Gilbert's fascinating Lacanian analysis in "Unnatural Mothers and Monstrous Children" of this childbirth links the monstrous child to the lack of the father. Gilbert, while calling the conversion and color change of the father deeply racist (336), does not note the fear of miscegenation that the text, and particularly the princess's dream, implies.

27. "Þan wist sche wele in her þouyt, / Þat on Mahoun leued he nouyt, / For changed was his hewe" (937–39).

28. Two disparate thirteenth-century manuscripts of this story, both in the Bibliothèque nationale de France, are edited in Brunel, *La fille du comte de Pontieu*. In the citations that follow, manuscript BnF fr. 770 is denoted I, and BnF fr. 12203 is denoted II. Translations are my own.

29. "Il n'avoit point d'oir de sa char" (II 4–5).

30. See Makeieff, "*La Fille du Comte de Ponthieu*: Edition and Study." Makeieff's edition is of the oldest surviving manuscript, BnF fr. 25462.

31. "Ele vit bien ke mieus li venoit faire par amours ke par force, se li manda ke ele le feroit. Quant ele fu renoïe et ele ot relenquie sa loy, li soudans le prist a feme a l'ussage et a le maniere de la tiere de Sarrazins" (II 357–61). Sharon Kinoshita in "The Romance of MiscegeNation," 121, has read this behavior as potential playacting on the part of the *fille*.

32. The thirteenth-century manuscripts diverge in wording here (Brunel, *La fille*, 39): "Quant il oïrent chou, si furent molt lié, et si firent sanllant d'umelier vers li, et ele leur desfendi et dist: 'Je sui Sarrasine, et si vous pri que de cose que vous aiés oïe nul plus biau sanllant n'en faites'" (I 493–97) [When they heard that, they were very happy and so started to humble themselves before her, and she refused to let them do that and said, "I am Saracen, and so I ask you because of what you have heard that you not make any further noble gesture"], while the second reads, "Et quant il oïrent çou, si en furent mout liét, et en fisent mout grant joie, et s'umelierent viers li. Elle lor desfendi k'il n'en fesissent nul samblant et dist: 'Jou sui Sarrazine renoïe, car autrement ne pooie durer, car jou fuisse piech'a morte, mais or vous prie jou et chasti, si chier com vous avés vos vies et houneurs a avoir greignours ke vous eustes onques, ke

pour cose ke vous aiiés veue ne oïe nul plus biel samblant n'en faites'" (II 609–17) [And when they heard that they were very happy about it and made great joy and humbled themselves toward her. She told them not to do it in any way and said, "I am a renounced Saracen, for otherwise I would not survive, thus I am a mortal sinner, thus I beg you and chasten you, so dear are your lives and honors to have greater than you ever were, that for this reason that you have seen or heard, do not make a grander gesture"].

33. Brunel, *La fille*, 45, reads "[Li Apostoiles] reconcilia la dame et remist en droite crestientét" [The legate reconciled the lady and returned her to proper Christianity]. Were she not truly Muslim, she would not need to reconvert.

34. In Brunel, *La fille*, 44, she says to her husand and father, "jou ai mout mesfait enviers le soudan car jou li ai tolu mon cors et son fil k'il mout amoit" (II 705–7) [I have done a great misdeed to the sultan because I took from him my body and my son whom he loved greatly].

35. "La dame qui feme estoit au soudant estoit la, et se le vit et li atenri li cuers, et dist: 'Sire, je sai françois, si parleroie a cest povre home, se vos plaisoit'" (I 348–50) [The lady who was the sultan's wife was there and saw him and softened her heart to him and said, "Sir, I know French and so I will speak to this poor man, if it please you"].

36. "La dame dont vous avés oï, ki estoit fille le conte et feme a cel soudan, estoit en la place u on en mena le conte, ki ses peres estoit, pour ocire. Lués ke ele l'ot veu, se li mua li sans et li cuers li atenri, ne mie por çou ke ele le couneust, fors tant ke Nature l'en destraignoit, et dist la dame au soudan: 'Sire, jou sui françoise, si parleroie mout volentiers a cel povre homme ansçois ke il morust, s'il vous plaisoit'" (II 451–57) [The lady about whom you have heard, who was the count's daughter and the sultan's wife, was in the place where they brought the count, her father, in order to kill him. As soon as she saw him, her mind and heart softened, not at all because she recognized him, so much had Nature distanced her from the matter. The lady said to the sultan, "Sir, I am French and I would most gladly speak to this poor man before he dies, if it be pleasing to you"].

37. Brunel, *La fille*, 41. This phrase is difficult to render into idiomatic English. It is the place where Nature intended for her to be.

38. Kinoshita in "The Romance of MiscegeNation," 125, sees Guillaume as different from his mother—he retains the taint of Saracen blood, while

she is able to integrate into either culture without problem. Yet she likewise seems to retain her Christian heritage, drawn inexplicably to her "terre de droite nature." While Kinoshita notes that Guillaume does not receive the inheritance he is due, she still sees this period as a golden age of medieval acculturation and finds that *La fille* participates in a pre-Eurocentric order (126).

39. "Et pour cesti aventure mains en ama sa fille, ki demouree li estoit, et mains l'ounora, et nanpourquant la damoisele devint mout sage et crut en grant sens, ensi ke tout l'amoient et prisoient por les biens ke on en disoit" (II 744–47).

40. Cord Whitaker in "Race and Conversion" also finds this sort of reasoning in the story of Custance, discussed below.

41. Each landless knight had been offered a boon due to his loyal fighting, and each said he wanted nothing other than the hand of his lord's daughter.

42. "Li soudans estut et pensa, et vit bien ke Malakins estoit preus et sages et bien poroit encore venir a grant houneur et a grant bien, et ke bien i seroit fille emploiee, se li dist: 'Malakin, par ma loy, vous m'avés grant cose requise, cor jou aim mout ma fille et plus n'ai d'oirs, si comme vous savés bien, et voirs est ke ele est nee et estraite des plus hautes gens et des plus vaillans de Franche, car estes vaillans et mout bien savés servir, jou le vous donrai volentiers, s'ele le veut'" (II 796–805) [The sultan stood there and thought and realized that Malaquin was noble and wise and could very well come to great honor and wealth, and that his daughter could be well used there, and so he said, "Malaquin, by my command, you have asked me a great favor, for I love my daughter greatly and have no other heir, as you well know. You see very well that she is born and descended from the most noble and valiant French families. Since you are valiant and know how to serve well, I will give her to you willingly if she wants it"].

43. For more on this, see Tolan, *Sons of Ishmael*, esp. "The Image of Saladin in the West," 79–101.

44. Kinoshita, "The Romance of MiscegeNation," 118.

45. de Weever, *Sheba's Daughters*, esp. chap. 1, "Whitening the Saracen: The Erasure of Alterity."

46. Sénac, *L'image de l'autre*, 63–73. He writes that "dans la seconde moité du XIIIe siècle, l'utilisation de la couleur noire devient prépondérante" (71). This is, of course, also the finding of Devisse, cited in chapter 2.

47. Or it could suggest an improvement in artistic technique.

48. "Ist zwîvel herzen nâchgebûr, daz muoz der sêle werden sûr. ges-maehet unde gezieret ist, swâ sich parrieret unverzaget mannes muot, als agelstern varwe tuot. der mac dennoch wesen geil: wand an im sint beidiu teil, des himels und der helle. der unstaete geselle hât die swarzen varwe gar, und wirt och nâch der vinster var: sô habet sich an die blanken der mit staeten gedanken" (I.1.1–14). All citations of Wolfram's *Parzival* are from Karl Lachmann's 1891 edition, with English renderings from the 1961 translation by Helen M. Mustard and Charles E. Passage.

49. "Liute vinster sô diu naht wârn alle die von Zazamanc: bî den dûht in diu wîle lanc. doch hiez er herberge nemen: des moht och si vil wol gezemen, daz se im die besten gâben" (I.17.24–29).

This repulsion toward black skin is echoed later in the book. When the ladies of Arthur's court encounter Feirefiz, they are reluctant to kiss him at first and send women of lesser rank to test the waters. Parzival's own children refuse at first to kiss their uncle, citing fear of his mottled skin (I.16.805–6).

50. Wolfram, *Parzival*, I.1.20.

51. "ist iht liehters denne der tac, dem glîchet niht diu künegin. si hete wîplîchen sin, und was abr anders rîterlîch, der touwegen rôsen ungelîch. nâch swarzer varwe was ir schîn" (I.24.6–11).

52. "der küneginne rîche ir ougen fuogten hôhen pîn, dô si gesach den Anschevîn. der was sô minneclîche gevar, daz er entslôz ir herze gar, ez waere ir liep oder leit" (I.23.22–27).

53. "aldâ wîp unde man verjach, sine gesaehn nie helt sô wünneclîch; ir gote im solten sîn gelîch" (I.36.18–20).

54. "er was gein valscher fuore ein tôr, in swarzer varwe als ich ein Môr" (I.26.21–22).

55. "Gahmureten dûhte sân, swie si waere ein heidenin, mit triwen wîplîcher sin in wîbes herze nie geslouf. ir kiusche was ein reiner touf, und ouch der regen der sie begôz, der wâc der von ir ougen flôz ûf ir zobel und an ir brust. riwen phlege was ir gelust, und rehtiu jâmers lêre" (I.28.10–19).

56. "Als ein agelster wart gevar sîn hâr und och sîn vel vil gar" (I.57.27–28).

57. "diu küngîn kust in sunder twâl vil dicke an sîniu blanken mâl" (I.57.19–20).

58. Wolfram, *Parzival*, XVI.16.813.

59. John Tolan gives the context for this debate and further reading in *Petrus Alfonsi*, 117.

60. Duggan, "'For Force Is Not of God'?"

61. See Ramey, "Jean Bodel's Jeu," for a discussion of this conversion and the problem of crusade.

62. The story of Guillaume and Orable is found in the Guillaume d'Orange cycle, principally in *La Prise d'Orange*. See Lachet's modern French–Old French edition.

63. *Bevis of Hampton*, line 523.

64. Peggy McCracken in *The Curse of Eve*, 105, notes that converted Saracen women are allowed entrance into the genealogy of the Grail guardians, but women are allowed less and less control over the Grail as it becomes associated with Eucharistic ritual.

65. "cristned never so white" (355). In "Race and Conversion," 228, Cord Whitaker uses the perspective of the sultaness to argue persuasively for a genealogy of blood. For Whitaker, the possibility of a true and full, permanent conversion would eliminate racism. This tale, for me, shows that conversion is not the question. Some people and places are more acceptable than others. Custance cannot fathom living among Syrians, even if they are Christianized.

66. Whitaker suggests this is facilitated by the fact that Northumbria, the area of England where Custance lands, was Christian in the past, so there is evidence of God's grace in Alla's genealogy ("Race and Conversion," 215). This raises the question of why past conversion would provide grace for Northumbria but current conversion would not do so for Syria. Whitaker goes on to name, correctly I think, race (for him read as blood) as the real issue (216).

Carolyn Dinshaw also remarks on the instability of religion in this tale as well as on mother-son incest, which she links to paleness, in "Pale Faces," 26–29. While both mothers attempt to foil their sons' marriages to Custance, the mothers seem more motivated by concerns about offspring (appropriate grandchildren) than by jealousy, a position echoed by Heng in *Empire of Magic* and by Whitaker.

67. Heng, *Empire of Magic*, 233.

68. Scholars date the *Chanson de Guillaume* from about the same time as the *Chanson de Roland*. This dating may be complicated by a nineteenth-century desire to privilege Charlemagne over Guillaume. There are many more editions and translations of the Roland story than the Guillaume story, though editions are available for both.

69. Orable/Guibourc was married to the Saracen Thibaut, but she en-

sorcelled him nightly, turning him into a golden apple. She gave him fantastic sex dreams, and she slept peacefully, preserving her virginity for Guillaume, whom she already loved.

70. Not possible, of course, if Orable did not consummate her marriage with Thibaut, but these Medea-like images surround her, much like the Medea-like bride that Apponius imagined in his commentary on the Song of Songs.

71. At the same time that he notes the importance of the sociopolitical themes of romance epic, William Calin claims that the love of "la belle Sarrasine" functions as a parody of *la fin'amor* ("Textes médiévaux et tradition," 15). This reading is echoed by others, not only in the case of *Prise d'Orange*, but also for the twelfth-century chantefable *Aucassin et Nicolette* and other texts that present cultural miscegenation. Tony Hunt suggests that Aucassin et Nicolette is a parody as well, in "La parodie médiévale." Rather than seeing these romance epics as "epic lite," I suggest that they do important cultural work imagining a multicultural, multiracial society.

72. One is reminded here of the 2012 comments of Missouri congressman Todd Akin, who suggested that in cases of "legitimate rape" a woman's body had ways of shutting down the reproductive process.

73. See note 46.

Chapter 5. Mapping the Monstrous

1. Lestringant, *Mapping the Renaissance World*, 12.

2. Susan K. Kevra (private communication) pointed out that the crosses could equally well indicate, not the limit of knowledge, but the beginning of knowledge about the New World. Indeed, the crosses seem to challenge the next explorer to go yet farther, while the monstrous races on a medieval map may have served to warn travelers not to visit certain areas. I find it likely that historical medieval travelers were drawn to the margins of the known world, seeking out these races from sheer curiosity.

3. Lestringant, *Mapping the Renaissance World*, 12.

4. Edmund S. Morgan in *American Heroes*, 20–23, discusses Columbus's inability to "see" the New World clearly because of undue influence from books, namely those of Pliny, Marco Polo, and Mandeville.

5. This idea is so prevalent in Western thought that one science writer suggests that it has unduly influenced current research on human evolu-

tion; see Nee, "Great Chain," 429. For a detailed analysis of the history and importance of the chain of being, see Lovejoy, *Great Chain*.

6. Augustine, *City of God*, chap. 16.

7. Ibid., 16.8.

8. "The diversity of languages arose with the building of the Tower after the Flood, for before the pride of that Tower divided human society . . ." (9.i.1) and "We have treated languages first, and then nations, because nations arose from languages, and not languages from nations" (9.i.14). All citations of Isidore, *Etymologies*, are from the 2006 translation by Barney et al.

9. Ibid., 9.ii.2–4.

10. Ibid., 9.ii.104–7.

11. Ibid., 9.ii.120–22.

12. Ibid., 7.vi.13–16.

13. Pliny, *Naturalis historia*, 7.26.

14. Cited in Friedman, *Monstrous Races*, 192, emphasis mine. For a full treatment of the work, see Albert the Great, *Questions*.

15. For details on this discussion, see Koch, "Sind die Pygmäen Menschen?" An excellent overview of Peter of Auvergne's disputations or debates is found in Schabel, "Quodlibeta."

16. Schabel, "Quodlibeta," 210.

17. Translated with reference to Lecoq, "La 'Mappemonde,'" 20. The original is found in the Patrologia Latina 176, col. 677D–678AB. See also the introduction and commentary to Hugh, *Descriptio*, by Patrick Gautier Dalché.

18. The command to go forth, convert, and baptize all the nations of the world is taken from Matthew 28:19–20.

19. Long, introduction, 2.

20. For a concise overview of the importance of Bartholomew's work, see Long, introduction; Seymour et al., *Bartholomaeus*; Steele, *Mediaeval Lore*.

21. The pygmies are described in book 15, chapter 120 ("De Pigmea"), where the inhabitants of the regions of the world are described, as well as in book 18, chapter 86 ("De pigmeis"), on animals. For an accessible edition, see Bartholomaeus, *Properties of Things*, 797, 1236–37.

22. Odoric, *Travels*, 113.

23. Ibid., 114.

24. Augustine, *City of God*, chaps. 14, 17. Also see Friedman, *Monstrous Races*, 255n29.

25. Odoric, *Travels*, 129.

26. Ibid., 130.

27. Ibid., 149.

28. Ibid., 131–32.

29. Mandeville, *Travels*, 145.

30. Ibid., 145–46.

31. Cosa, *Mappamundi*.

32. McIntosh, *Piri Reis Map*, 72.

33. Inan, *Life and Works of Pirî Reis*, 30–31.

34. Cartier, *Voyages*, 37.

35. Ibid., 131.

36. Desceliers, *Mariner's Guide*. See also Burden, *Mapping of North America*.

37. Cartier, *Voyages*, 135.

38. Ibid., 144.

39. Sepúlveda, "Democrates Alter."

40. Ibid., 495–96.

41. Gliozzi, *Adam et le Nouveau Monde*, 243–58.

42. BBC, "Pygmy Artists."

Chapter 6. Conclusions

1. On this topic, see Ramey and Pugh, *Race, Class, and Gender in "Medieval" Cinema*, and Kelly and Pugh, *Queer Movie Medievalisms*. For a more general study of cinematic medievalism, including modern anxieties that find their way into these films, see Finke and Shichtman, *Cinematic Illuminations*.

2. Pao, "Recasting Race," 1–2.

3. Ibid., 3.

4. Ibid., 10. Pao goes on to show that the ability to mount color-blind productions as well as the desirability of such productions has been seriously called into question.

5. Ibid., 17.

6. I use this anachronism intentionally, as Pugh and I did in *Race, Class, and Gender in "Medieval" Cinema*. We maintain that medieval cinema refers to a specific genre of anachronistic films.

7. Azeem's sensitivity to women is in ironic contrast to the prevalent post-9/11 American attitudes about Islam and the position of women.

8. For more on this, see the excellent article by Finke and Shichtman, "Inner-City Chivalry." Finke and Shichtman point to the various references throughout the film to the LA riots, including street signs, dialogue, and situations that, while the viewer does not need to "get" all of the references, illustrate the deeper message Junger has. The viewers that belong to the communities directly affected by the riots would notice and appreciate more of the the the multiple layers of meaning.

9. Desrues, "Entretien," 15. "C'est dans la mesure où il constitue une époque charnière que le Moyen Age m'a intéressé avec toujours la perspective de travailler sur l'Histoire, d'aller le plus loin possible dans la mémoire de mes contemporains pour leur donner à voir leurs origines historiques et culturelles en établissant sans cesse le parallèle avec la société dans laquelle ils vivent."

10. Bertin-Maghit, "Trois cinéastes," 112. "une reconstruction subjective de l'Histoire qui entre en résonance avec notre présent."

11. Ibid., 109.

12. Turoldus is the name given at the end of the Oxford *Roland*. While we do not know Turoldus's actual role in writing the story, he apparently communicated the story in this particular manuscript as a scribe or storyteller.

13. "Ce qui m'intéresse c'est de parler du présent et dans ce présent il y a . . . la difficulté de faire des films." Desrues, "Entretien," 19.

14. Desrues, "La Chanson de Roland," 102; Oudart, "Le P.C.F."; Bertin-Maghit, "Trois cinéastes," 116.

15. Bertin-Maghit, "Trois cinéastes," 112.

16. Ibid. "L'épopée de Roland et de Charlemagne a marqué ma scolarité en Algérie, où dans le contexte de la guerre, j'ai ressenti la dimension raciste du texte. Il était difficile de ne pas faire un rapport entre la guerre de Roland, ses visées imperialists et la guerre colonialiste."

17. Fanon, *Wretched of the Earth*, 3.

18. Ibid., 23.

19. Desrues, "Entretien," 18.

Bibliography

Akbari, Suzanne Conklin. "From Due East to True North." In *The Postco-lonial Middle Ages*, edited by Jeffrey Jerome Cohen, 19–34. New York: St. Martin's Press, 2000.

Albert the Great. *Questions concerning Aristotle's "On Animals."* Translated by Irven M. Resnick and Kenneth F. Kitchell Jr. Washington, D.C.: Catholic University of America Press, 2008.

Alleyne, Mervyn C. *The Construction and Representation of Race and Ethnicity in the Caribbean and the World.* Kingston: University of the West Indies Press, 2002.

Appiah, Kwame Anthony. "Race." In *Critical Terms for Literary Study*, edited by Frank Lentricchia and Tom McLaughlin, 274–87. Chicago: University of Chicago Press, 1989.

Apponius. *Commentaire sur le Cantique des cantiques.* Edited and translated by Bernard de Vregille and Louis Neyrand. 3 vols. Paris: Éditions du Cerf, 1997–98.

Aristotle. *Generation of Animals.* Translated by A. L. Peck. Cambridge, Mass.: Harvard University Press, 1943.

Astell, Ann W. *The Song of Songs in the Middle Ages.* Ithaca, N.Y.: Cornell University Press, 1990.

Atkinson, Clarissa W. *The Oldest Vocation: Christian Motherhood in the Middle Ages.* Ithaca, N.Y.: Cornell University Press, 1991.

Augustine. *The City of God against the Pagans.* Translated by R. W. Dyson. Cambridge: Cambridge University Press, 1998.

Baldwin, John W. *The Language of Sex: Five Voices from Northern France around 1200.* Chicago: University of Chicago Press, 1994.

Bale, Anthony. *The Jew in the Medieval Book: English Antisemitisms, 1350–1500.* Cambridge: Cambridge University Press, 2007.

Balibar, Étienne. "Sub specie universitatis." *Topoi* 25 (2006): 3–16.

Banton, Michael. *Racial Theories*. Cambridge: Cambridge University Press, 1998.

Barot, Odysse, Eugène Yung, and Émile Alglave. *Revue des cours littéraires de la France et de l'étranger*. 7 vols. Paris: Germer Baillière, 1863–1870.

Bartholomaeus Anglicus. *On the Properties of Soul and Body = De proprietatibus rerum, libri III et IV*. Edited by R. James Long. Toronto: Pontifical Institute of Mediaeval Studies, 1979.

——. *On the Properties of Things: John Trevisa's Translation of Bartholomaeus Anglicus, De Proprietatibus Rerum*. Edited by M. C. Seymour et al. 3 vols. Oxford: Clarendon, 1975–78.

Bartlett, Robert. "The Face of the Barbarian." Chapter 6 of *Gerald of Wales, 1146–1223*. Oxford: Clarendon, 1982.

——. "Illustrating Ethnicity in the Middle Ages." In Eliav-Feldon, Isaac, and Ziegler, *Origins of Racism in the West*, 132–56.

BBC. "Pygmy Artists Housed in Congo Zoo." 13 July 2007. news.bbc.co.uk/2/hi/6898241.stm.

Belcher, Wendy Laura. "From Sheba They Come: Medieval Ethiopian Myth, US Newspapers, and a Modern American Narrative." *Callaloo* 33, no. 1 (2010): 239–57.

Bernard of Clairvaux. *On the Song of Songs I*. Vol. 1 of *The Works of Bernard of Clairvaux*. Translated by Kilian Walsh. Kalamazoo, Mich.: Cistercian Publications, 2005.

Bertin-Maghit, Jean-Pierre. "Trois cinéastes en quête de l'histoire: Entretien avec René Allio, Frank Cassenti et Bertrand Tavernier." *Image et son: Revue de cinéma* 352 (1980): 108–17.

Bevis of Hampton. In *Four Romances of England*. Edited by Ronald B. Herzman, Graham Drake, and Eve Salisbury. Kalamazoo, Mich.: Medieval Institute Publications, 1999.

Bhabha, Homi K. *The Location of Culture*. London: Routledge, 2004.

——. "Of Mimicry and Man: The Ambivalence of Colonial Discourse." *October* 28 (1984): 125–33.

Biddick, Kathleen. *The Shock of Medievalism*. Durham, N.C.: Duke University Press, 1998.

Blamires, Alcuin. *The Case for Women in Medieval Culture*. Oxford: Clarendon, 1997.

——, ed. *Woman Defamed and Woman Defended: An Anthology of Medieval Texts*. Oxford: Clarendon, 1992.

Bloch, R. Howard. *Medieval Misogyny and the Invention of Western Romantic Love*. Chicago: University of Chicago Press, 1991.

Bloch, R. Howard, and Stephen G. Nichols, eds. *Medievalism and the Modernist Temper*. Baltimore: Johns Hopkins University Press, 1996.

Blumenbach, Johann Friedrich. *On the Natural Varieties of Mankind = De generis humani varietate nativa*. Translated by Thomas Bendyshe. New York: Bergmann, 1969.

Boccaccio, Giovanni. *Concerning Famous Women*. Translated by Guido A. Guarino. New Brunswick, N.J.: Rutgers University Press, 1963.

Boulle, Pierre H. "François Bernier and the Origins of the Modern Concept of Race." In *The Color of Liberty: Histories of Race in France*, edited by Sue Peabody and Tyler Stovall, 11–27. Durham, N.C.: Duke University Press, 2003.

Bowden, Mary Weatherspoon. *Washington Irving*. Boston: Twayne, 1981.

Brodkin, Karen. *How Jews Became White Folks and What That Says About Race in America*. New Brunswick, N.J.: Rutgers University Press, 1998.

Brunel, Clovis, ed. *La fille du comte de Pontieu: Nouvelle du XIIIe siècle*. Paris: Champion, 1926.

Budge, E. A. Wallis, ed. and trans. *The Queen of Sheba and Her Only Son Menyelek: The Kebra Nagast*. 1922. London: Kegan Paul, 2001.

Burde, Mark. "The Song of Roland in Nineteenth-Century France." In *Approaches to Teaching the "Song of Roland,"* edited by William W. Kibler and Leslie Zarker Morgan, 124–32. New York: MLA, 2006.

Burden, Philip D. *The Mapping of North America: A List of Printed Maps, 1511–1670*. Rickmansworth, Herts.: Raleigh, 1996.

Burgess, Glyn S., and Clara Strijbosch, eds. *The Brendan Legend: Texts and Versions*. Leiden: Brill, 2006.

Burland, Margaret Jewett. *Strange Words: Retelling and Reception in the Medieval Roland Textual Tradition*. Notre Dame, Ind.: University of Notre Dame Press, 2007.

Bynum, Caroline Walker. *The Resurrection of the Body in Western Christianity, 200–1336*. New York: Columbia University Press, 1995.

Byron, Gay L. *Symbolic Blackness and Ethnic Difference in Early Christian Literature*. New York: Routledge, 2002.

Cadden, Joan. *Meanings of Sex Difference in the Middle Ages: Medicine, Science, and Culture*. Cambridge: Cambridge University Press, 1993.

Caferro, William. *Contesting the Renaissance*. Malden, Mass.: Wiley-Blackwell, 2011.

Calin, William. "Textes médiévaux et tradition: La chanson de geste est-elle une épopée?" In *Romance Epic: Essays on a Medieval Literary Genre*, edited by Hans-Erich Keller, 11–19. Kalamazoo, Mich.: Medieval Institute Publications, 1987.

Campbell, Kofi Omoniyi Sylvanus. *Literature and Culture in the Black Atlantic: From Pre- to Postcolonial.* New York: Palgrave Macmillan, 2006

Campbell, Mary B. *The Witness and the Other World: Exotic European Travel Writing, 400–1600.* Ithaca, N.Y.: Cornell University Press, 1988.

Cartier, Jacques. *The Voyages of Jacques Cartier.* Translated by Henry P. Biggar. Introduction by Ramsay Cook. Toronto: University of Toronto Press, 1993.

Chazan, Robert. *Medieval Stereotypes and Modern Antisemitism.* Berkeley: University of California Press, 1997.

Clapp, Nicholas. *Sheba: Through the Desert in Search of the Legendary Queen.* Boston: Houghton Mifflin, 2001.

Cohen, Jeffrey Jerome. *Hybridity, Identity, and Monstrosity in Medieval Britain: On Difficult Middles.* New York: Palgrave Macmillan, 2006.

Cortés Vázquez, Luis, ed. *La chanson de Roland.* Translated by Paulette Gabaudan. Paris: Nizet, 1994.

Cosa, Juan de la. *Mappamundi.* Paint on parchment, 1500. Museo Naval, Madrid.

Crawford, O.G.S. *Ethiopian Itineraries, Circa 1400–1524.* London: Hakluyt Society, 1958.

Dayan, Colin. *The Law Is a White Dog: How Legal Rituals Make and Unmake Persons.* Princeton, N.J.: Princeton University Press, 2011.

Delacampagne, Christian. *L'invention du racisme: Antiquité et Moyen Âge.* Paris: Fayard, 1983.

———. "Racism and the West: From Praxis to Logos." In Goldberg, *Anatomy of Racism*, 83–88.

Desceliers, Pierre. *A Mariner's Guide to the New World.* New York: American Heritage, 1957.

DeSimone, Russell J. *The Bride and the Bridegroom of the Fathers: An Anthology of Patristic Interpretations of the Song of Songs.* Rome: Istituto Patristico Augustinianum, 2000.

Desrues, Hubert. "La Chanson de Roland." *Image et son: Revue de cinéma* 331 (1978): 101–2.

———. "La Chanson de Roland: Entretien avec Frank Cassenti." *Image et son: Revue de cinéma* 328 (1978): 15–19.

Devisse, Jean, ed. *From the Early Christian Era to the "Age of Discovery."* Vol. 2 of *The Image of the Black in Western Art*, edited by David Bindman and Henry Louis Gates Jr. Cambridge, Mass.: Belknap Press, 2010.

de Weever, Jacqueline. *Sheba's Daughters: Whitening and Demonizing the Saracen Woman in Medieval French Epic*. London: Routledge, 1998.

Dinshaw, Carolyn. "Pale Faces: Race, Religion, and Affect in Chaucer's Texts and Their Readers." *Studies in the Age of Chaucer: The Yearbook of the New Chaucer Society* 23 (2001): 19–41.

Dobie, Madeleine. *Trading Places: Colonization and Slavery in Eighteenth-Century French Culture*. Ithaca, N.Y.: Cornell University Press, 2010.

Douay-Rheims Catholic Bible. drbo.org.

Dubois, Laurent. *A Colony of Citizens: Revolution & Slave Emancipation in the French Caribbean, 1787–1804*. Chapel Hill, N.C.: University of North Carolina Press, 2006.

Duggan, Lawrence G. "'For Force Is Not of God'? Compulsion and Conversion from Yahweh to Charlemagne." In Muldoon, *Varieties of Religious Conversion*, 49–62.

Eliav-Feldon, Miriam, Benjamin Isaac, and Joseph Ziegler, eds. *The Origins of Racism in the West*. Cambridge: Cambridge University Press, 2009.

Emery, Elizabeth, and Laura Morowitz. *Consuming the Past: The Medieval Revival in Fin-de-Siècle France*. Burlington, Vt.: Ashgate, 2003.

Evans, E. P. *The Criminal Prosecution and Capital Punishment of Animals*. London: W. Heinemann, 1906.

Fanon, Frantz. *The Wretched of the Earth*. Translated by Constance Farrington. New York: Grove, 1963.

Fellous, Sonia. *Histoire de la Bible de Moïse Arragel, Tolède 1422–1433: Quand un rabbin interprète la Bible pour les Chrétiens*. Paris: Somogy éditions d'art, 2001.

Ferrante, Joan. "Public Postures and Private Maneuvers: Roles Medieval Women Play." In *Women and Power in the Middle Ages*, edited by Mary Erler and Maryanne Kowaleski, 213–29. Athens: University of Georgia Press, 1988.

Finke, Laurie A., and Martin B. Shichtman. *Cinematic Illuminations: The Middle Ages on Film*. Baltimore: Johns Hopkins University Press, 2010.

———. "Inner-City Chivalry in Gil Junger's *Black Knight*: A South Central Yankee in King Leo's Court." In Ramey and Pugh, *Race, Class, and Gender in "Medieval" Cinema*, 107–22.

Fischer, Sibylle. *Modernity Disavowed: Haiti and the Cultures of Slavery in the Age of Revolution*. Durham, N.C.: Duke University Press, 2004.

Fredrickson, George M. *Racism: A Short History*. Princeton, N.J.: Princeton University Press, 2003.

Freedman, Paul. *Images of the Medieval Peasant*. Stanford, Calif.: Stanford University Press, 1999.

Friedberg, E., and A. Richter. *Corpus iuris canonici*. 2 vols. Liepzig: Bernhard Tauchnitz, 1879–81.

Friedman, John Block. *The Monstrous Races in Medieval Art and Thought*. 1981. Syracuse, N.Y.: Syracuse University Press, 2000.

Gilbert, Jane. "Unnatural Mothers and Monstrous Children in *The King of Tars* and *Sir Gowther*." In *Medieval Women: Texts and Contexts in Late Medieval Britain: Essays for Felicity Riddy*, edited by Jocelyn Wogan-Browne et al., 329–44. Turnhout: Brepols, 2000.

Glacken, Clarence J. "Environmental Influences Within a Divinely Created World." In *Traces on the Rhodian Shore*, 254–87. Berkeley: University of California Press, 1967.

Gliozzi, Giuliano. *Adam et le Nouveau Monde: La naissance de l'anthropologie comme idéologie coloniale; Des généalogies bibliques aux théories raciales, 1500–1700*. Translated by Arlette Estève and Pascal Gabellone. Lecques, France: Théétète, 2000.

Goldberg, David Theo, ed. *Anatomy of Racism*. Minneapolis: University of Minnesota Press, 1990.

Goldenberg, David M. *The Curse of Ham: Race and Slavery in Early Judaism, Christianity, and Islam*. Princeton, N.J.: Princeton University Press, 2003.

———. "Racism, Color Symbolism, and Color Prejudice." In Eliav-Feldon, Isaac, and Ziegler, *The Origins of Racism in the West*, 88–108.

Gormont et Isembart. Edited by Alphonse Bayot. Brussels: Revues des bibliothèques et archives de Belgique, 1906.

Gould, Stephen Jay. *The Mismeasure of Man*. Rev. ed. New York: Norton, 1996.

Graham, John M. "National Identity and the Politics of Publishing the Troubadours." In Bloch and Nichols, *Medievalism and the Modernist Temper*, 59–74.

Guzman, Gregory. "The Encyclopedist Vincent of Beauvais and His Mongol Extracts from John of Plano Carpini and Simon of Saint-Quentin." *Speculum* 49 (1974): 287–307.

Halter, Marek. *Zipporah, Wife of Moses: A Novel.* Translated by Howard Curtis. New York: Crown, 2005.

Hannaford, Ivan. *Race: The History of an Idea in the West.* Baltimore: Johns Hopkins University Press, 1996.

Hearn, M. F., ed. *The Architectural Theory of Viollet-le-Duc: Readings and Commentary.* Cambridge, Mass.: MIT Press, 1990.

Hendrix, James P., Jr. "A New Vision of America: Lewis and Clark and the Emergence of the American Imagination." *Great Plains Quarterly* 21 (2001): 211–32.

Heng, Geraldine. *Empire of Magic: Medieval Romance and the Politics of Cultural Fantasy.* New York: Columbia University Press, 2003.

———. "The Invention of Race in the European Middle Ages." Part I, "Race Studies, Modernity, and the Middle Ages"; part II, "Locations of Medieval Race." *Literature Compass* 8, no. 5 (2011): 258–74, 275–93.

Hourihane, Colum. *Pontius Pilate, Anti-Semitism, and the Passion in Medieval Art.* Princeton, N.J.: Princeton University Press, 2009.

Hugh of Saint-Victor. *La "Descriptio mappe mundi" de Hugues de Saint-Victor.* Edited by Patrick Gautier Dalché. Paris: Études augustiniennes, 1988.

Hult, David F. "Gaston Paris and the Invention of Courtly Love." In Bloch and Nichols, *Medievalism and the Modernist Temper,* 192–224.

Hunt, Tony. "La parodie médiévale: Le cas d'Aucassin et Nicolette." *Romania* 100 (1979): 341–81.

Inan, Âfet. *Life and Works of Pirî Reis: The Oldest Map of America.* Ankara: Turkish Historical Association, 1954.

Irving, Washington. *The Alhambra.* Philadelphia: Carey & Lea, 1832.

———. *The Alhambra.* Illustrated by Felix Octavius Carr Darley. New York: G. P. Putnam, 1851.

———. *The Alhambra.* Introduction by Ángel Flores. Illustrated by Lima de Freitas. Mount Vernon, N.Y.: printed for the Limited Editions Club by A. Colish, 1969.

———. *The Alhambra.* Introduction by Andrew B. Myers. Illustrated by F.O.C. Darley. Tarrytown, N.Y.: Sleepy Hollow Press, 1982.

———. *Astoria; or, Anecdotes of an Enterprise Beyond the Rocky Mountains.* 1836. Norman: University of Oklahoma Press, 1964.

Isidore. *The Etymologies of Isidore of Seville.* Translated by Stephen A. Barney, W. J. Lewis, J. A. Beach, and Oliver Berghof. Cambridge: Cambridge University Press, 2006.

————. *The Medical Writings*. Edited and translated by William D. Sharpe. Philadelphia: American Philosophical Society, 1964.

Jeanroy, A. "Boccace, Christine de Pizan, le *De claris mulieribus*, principale source du *Livre de la Cité des Dames*." *Romania* 48 (1922): 93–105.

Jordan, Constance. "Boccaccio's In-Famous Women: Gender and Civic Virtue in the *De Mulieribus Claris*." In *Ambiguous Realities: Women in the Middle Ages and Renaissance*, edited by Carole Levin and Jeanie Watson, 25–47. Detroit: Wayne State University Press, 1987.

Jordan, William Chester. "Why Race?" *Journal of Medieval and Early Modern Studies* 31, no. 1 (2001): 165–74.

Josephus, Flavius. *Jewish Antiquities*. Vol. 1 (books 1–3) translated by Henry St. John Thackeray; vol. 3 (books 8–9) translated by Ralph Marcus. Loeb Classical Library. Cambridge, Mass.: Harvard University Press, 1998.

Kappler, Claude. *Monstres, démons, et merveilles à la fin du Moyen Âge: Le regard de l'histoire*. Paris: Payot, 1980.

Kelly, Kathleen Coyne, and Tison Pugh. *Queer Movie Medievalisms*. Burlington, Vt.: Ashgate, 2009.

Kessler, Herbert L., and David Nirenberg, eds. *Judaism and Christian Art: Aesthetic Anxieties from the Catacombs to Colonialism*. Philadelphia: University of Pennsylvania Press, 2011.

The King of Tars. English Poetry Full-Text Database. Cambridge: Chadwyck-Healey, 1992.

Kinoshita, Sharon. "The Romance of MiscegeNation: Negotiating Identities in *La Fille du comte de Pontieu*." In *Postcolonial Moves: Medieval Through Modern*, edited by Patricia Clare Ingham and Michelle R. Warren, 111–32. New York: Palgrave, 2003.

Koch, Joseph. "Sind die Pygmäen Menschen?" *Archiv für Geschichte der Philosophie* 40, no. 2 (1931): 194–213.

Kraemer, Ross Shepard. *When Aseneth Met Joseph: A Late Antique Tale of the Biblical Patriarch and His Egyptian Wife, Reconsidered*. Oxford: Oxford University Press, 1998.

Lachet, Claude, ed. and trans. *La Prise d'Orange: Chanson de geste (fin XIIe–début XIIIe siècle)*. Paris: Champion, 2010.

Lampert, Lisa. "Race, Periodicity, and the (Neo-) Middle Ages." *Modern Language Quarterly: A Journal of Literary History* 65, no. 3 (2004): 391–421.

Lampert-Weissig, Lisa. *Medieval Literature and Postcolonial Studies*. Edinburgh: Edinburgh University Press, 2010.

Lang, Berel, ed. *Race and Racism in Theory and Practice*. Lanham, Md.: Rowman & Littlefield, 2000.

Laqueur, Thomas Walter. *Making Sex: Body and Gender from the Greeks to Freud*. Cambridge, Mass.: Harvard University Press, 1990.

Lasker, Daniel J. *Jewish Philosophical Polemics against Christianity in the Middle Ages*. New York: Ktav, 1977.

Lassner, Jacob. *Demonizing the Queen of Sheba: Boundaries of Gender and Culture in Postbiblical Judaism and Medieval Islam*. Chicago: University of Chicago Press, 1993.

Latin Vulgate Bible. drbo.org/lvb.

Leclercq, Jean. *Monks and Love in Twelfth-Century France*. New York: Oxford University Press, 1979.

Lecoq, Danielle. "La 'Mappemonde' du *De Arca Noe Mystica* de Hugues de Saint-Victor (1128–29)." In *Géographie du monde au Moyen Âge et à la Renaissance*, edited by Monique Pelletier, 9–31. Paris: Éditions du Comité des Travaux Historiques et Scientifiques, 1989.

LeMenager, Stephanie. "Trading Stories: Washington Irving and the Global West." *American Literary History* 15, no. 4 (2003): 683–708.

Lestringant, Frank. *Mapping the Renaissance World: The Geographical Imagination in the Age of Discovery*. Translated by David Fausett. Cambridge: Polity Press, 1994.

Lévi-Strauss, Claude. *Elementary Structures of Kinship*. Rev. ed. Translated by James Harle Bell, John Richard von Sturmer, and Rodney Needham, ed. Boston: Beacon Press, 1969.

Livre des merveilles: Marco Polo, Odoric de Pordenone, Mandeville, Hayton, etc. 2 vols. Paris: Berthaud, 1907.

Lombroso, Cesare. *Criminal Man*. Translated by Mary Gibson and Nicole Hahn Rafter. Durham, N.C.: Duke University Press, 2006.

Lomperis, Linda. "Medieval Travel Writing and the Question of Race." *Journal of Medieval and Early Modern Studies* 31, no. 1 (2001): 147–64.

Long, R. James. Introduction to Bartholomaeus Anglicus, *On the Properties of Soul and Body*.

Lovejoy, Arthur O. *The Great Chain of Being: A Study of the History of an Idea*. Cambridge, Mass.: Harvard University Press, 1936.

Maccoby, Hyam, ed. and trans. *Judaism on Trial: Jewish-Christian Disputations in the Middle Ages*. Rutherford, N.J.: Fairleigh Dickinson University Press, 1982.

MacLehose, William F. "Nurturing Danger: High Medieval Medicine and

the Problem(s) of the Child." In *Medieval Mothering*, edited by John
Carmi Parsons and Bonnie Wheeler, 3–24. New York: Garland, 1996.

Makeieff, Jean-Pierre Serge. "*La Fille du Comte de Ponthieu*: Edition and
Study." Ph.D. diss., University of California, Berkeley, 2007.

Mandeville, John. *The Travels of Sir John Mandeville*. Translated by
C.W.R.D. Moseley. London: Penguin, 1983.

Marvels of the East: A Full Reproduction of the Three Known Copies. Edited
by Montague Rhodes James. Oxford: printed for the Roxburghe Club
by Oxford University Press, 1929.

Matter, E. Ann. *Voice of My Beloved: The Song of Songs in Western Medieval Christianity*. Philadelphia: University of Pennsylvania Press, 1990.

McCracken, Peggy. *The Curse of Eve, the Wound of the Hero: Blood, Gender, and Medieval Literature*. Philadelphia: University of Pennsylvania
Press, 2003.

McIntosh, Gregory C. *The Piri Reis Map of 1513*. Athens: University of
Georgia Press, 2000.

Miller, Christopher L. *The French Atlantic Triangle: Literature and Culture
of the Slave Trade*. Durham, N.C.: Duke University Press, 2008.

Moore, Megan. *Exchanges in Exoticism: Cross-Cultural Marriage and the
Making of the Mediterranean in Old French Romance*. Toronto: University of Toronto Press, 2014.

Morgan, Edmund S. *American Heroes: Profiles of Men and Women Who
Shaped Early America*. New York: Norton, 2009.

Muldoon, James. "Race or Culture: Medieval Notions of Difference." In
Lang, *Race and Racism in Theory and Practice*, 79–98.

———, ed. *Varieties of Religious Conversion in the Middle Ages*. Gainesville:
University Press of Florida, 1997.

Murphy, Kevin D. *Memory and Modernity: Viollet-le-Duc at Vézelay*. University Park: Pennsylvania State University Press, 2000.

Nee, Sean. "The Great Chain of Being." *Nature* 435, no. 7041 (2005): 429.

Nepaulsingh, Colbert. "The Continental Fallacy of Race." In Lang, *Race
and Racism in Theory and Practice*, 141–52.

Nicholas of Lyra. *The Postilla of Nicholas of Lyra on the Song of Songs*.
Edited and translated by James George Kiecker. Reformation Texts
with Translation (1350–1650). Milwaukee: Marquette University Press,
1998.

Nichols, Stephen G. "Modernism and the Politics of Medieval Studies."
In Bloch and Nichols, *Medievalism and the Modernist Temper*, 25–56.

Nilus. *Commentaire sur le Cantique des cantiques*. Edited by Marie-Gabrielle Guérard. Paris: Éditions du Cerf, 1994.

Nirenberg, David. *Anti-Judaism: The Western Tradition*. New York: Norton, 2013.

Odoric. *The Travels of Friar Odoric*. Translated by Henry Yule. Grand Rapids, Mich.: W. B. Eerdmans, 2002.

Omi, Michael, and Howard Winant. *Racial Formation in the United States: From the 1960s to the 1980s*. London: Routledge & Kegan Paul, 1986.

Origen. *Commentaire sur le Cantique des Cantiques*. Edited and translated by Luc Brésard, Henri Crouzel, and Marcel Borret. Paris: Éditions du Cerf, 1991.

Oudart, Jean-Pierre. "Le P.C.F. et la mode rétro: La Chanson de Roland." *Cahiers du cinéma* 295 (1978): 50–51.

Outlaw, Lucius. "Toward a Critical Theory of 'Race.'" In Goldberg, *Anatomy of Racism*, 58–82.

Pao, Angela C. "Recasting Race: Casting Practices and Racial Formation." *Theatre Survey* 41, no. 2 (2000): 1–22.

Paris, Gaston, and Ulysse Robert. *Miracles de Nostre Dame par personnages*. 8 vols. Paris: Firmin Didot, 1876–93.

Pizan, Christine de. *The Book of the City of Ladies*. Translated by Earl Jeffrey Richards. New York: Persea, 1982.

———. "The *Livre de la cité des dames* of Christine de Pisan: A Critical Edition." Edited by Maureen Cheney Curnow. Ph.D. diss., Vanderbilt University, 1975.

Pliny the Elder. *Naturalis historia*. 10 vols. Translated by Harris Rackham. Loeb Classical Library. Cambridge, Mass.: Harvard University Press, 1938–63.

Ramey, Lynn Tarte. *Christian, Saracen and Genre in Medieval French Literature*. New York: Routledge, 2001.

———. "Jean Bodel's Jeu de Saint Nicolas: A Call for Non-Violent Crusade." *French Forum* 27, no. 3 (2002).

Ramey, Lynn T., and Tison Pugh. *Race, Class, and Gender in "Medieval" Cinema*. New York: Palgrave Macmillan, 2007.

Rubin, Miri. *Gentile Tales: The Narrative Assault on Late Medieval Jews*. New Haven, Conn.: Yale University Press, 1999.

Ruggles, D. Fairchild. "Mothers of a Hybrid Dynasty: Race, Genealogy, and Acculturation in al-Andalus." *Journal of Medieval and Early Modern Studies* 34, no. 1 (2004): 65–94.

Schabel, Christopher. "The Quodlibeta of Peter of Auvergne." In *Theological Quodlibeta in the Middle Ages: The Fourteenth Century*, 80–130. Leiden: Brill, 2007.

Scraba, Jeffrey. "'Dear Old Romantic Spain': Washington Irving Imagines Andalucía." In *Romanticism and the Anglo-Hispanic Imaginary*, edited by Joselyn M. Almeida, 275–96. Amsterdam: Rodopi, 2010.

Sénac, Philippe. *L'image de l'autre: L'Occident medieval face à l'Islam*. Paris: Flammarion, 1983.

Sepúlveda, Juan Ginés de. "Democrates Alter." In *Introduction to Contemporary Civilization in the West*, prepared by Columbia College, 3d ed., 523–39. New York: Columbia University Press, 1960.

Seymour, M. C., et al. *Bartholomaeus Anglicus and His Encyclopaedia*. Brookfield, Vt.: Ashgate, 1992.

Shinan, Avigdor. "Moses and the Ethiopian Woman: Sources of a Story in the *Chronicles of Moses*." *Scripta Hierosolymitana* 27 (1978): 66–78.

Snowden, Frank M., Jr. *Before Color Prejudice: The Ancient View of Blacks*. Cambridge, Mass.: Harvard University Press, 1983.

Steel, Karl. *How to Make a Human: Animals and Violence in the Middle Ages*. Columbus: Ohio State University Press, 2011.

Steele, Robert. *Mediaeval Lore from Bartholomew Anglicus*. New York: Cooper Square, 1966.

Summerson, John. "Viollet-le-Duc and the Rational Point of View." In *Viollet-le-Duc*. London: Academy Editions, 1980.

Tate, Georges. *The Crusades and the Holy Land*. London: Thames and Hudson, 1996.

Tolan, John V. *Petrus Alfonsi and His Medieval Readers*. Gainesville: University Press of Florida, 1993.

———. *Sons of Ishmael: Muslims through European Eyes in the Middle Ages*. Gainesville: University Press of Florida, 2008.

Trachtenberg, Joshua. *The Devil and the Jews: The Medieval Conception of the Jew and Its Relation to Modern Anti-Semitism*. New Haven, Conn.: Yale University Press, 1943.

Valades, Didacus [Fray Diego Valadés]. *Rhetorica christiana ad concionandi et orandi usum accommodata . . .* Perugia: Pietro Giacomo Petrucci, 1579.

Vincent of Beauvais. *Speculum quadruplex sive Speculum maius*. 4 vols. Graz: Akademische Druck, 1965.

Viollet-le-Duc, Eugène-Emmanuel. *Dictionnaire raisonné de l'architecture française du XIe au XVIe siècle.* 10 vols. Paris: B. Bance and A. Morel, 1854–1868.

———. *The Habitations of Man in All Ages.* Translated by Benjamin Bucknall. Boston: J. R. Osgood, 1876.

———. *Histoire de l'habitation humaine.* Paris: Bibliothèque d'éducation et de récréation, 1875.

Whitaker, Cord. "Race and Conversion in Late Medieval England." Ph.D. diss., Duke University, 2009. dukespace.lib.duke.edu/dspace/bitstream/handle/10161/1653/D_Whitaker_Cord_a_200912.pdf?sequence=1.

Winslow, Karen S. "Moses' Cushite Marriage: Torah, Artapanus, and Josephus." In *Mixed Marriages: Intermarriage and Group Identity in the Second Temple Period,* edited by Christian Frevel, 280–302. New York: T & T Clark, 2011.

Wolfram von Eschenbach. *Parzival.* Edited by Karl Lachmann. Berlin: G. Reimer, 1891.

———. *Parzival.* Translated by Helen M. Mustard and Charles E. Passage. New York: Random House, 1961.

Wood, Michael. *In Search of Myths & Heroes: Exploring Four Epic Legends of the World.* Berkeley: University of California Press, 2005.

Zumthor, Paul. *Essai de poétique médiévale.* Paris: Seuil, 1972.

Index

Bhabha, Homi K., 31, 32

Bible, Biblical race and: Alba, *43*; Arragel, 43, 44; black characters in, 39, 63; cultural sharing in, 136n2; Douay-Rheims, 44–45, 137n3, 137n10; Hebrew, 49, 139n30; King James Version, 49, 139n30; Latin Vulgate, 49, 50, 137nn3–4, 137n10, 139n30; Middle Ages Catholic, 137n10; skin color in, 5, 131n1. *See also specific stories*

Biddick, Kathleen, 133n12

Black bride: double bind of, 47–54, 59–63; Jews as represented by, 52; of Moses, 39–42, *41*, 137nn3–4, 137n9; Neoplatonic model of, 53; Nilus's whitening of, 48–49; as Synagogue, 47. *See also* Song of Songs

Black Knight, 111, 114–18, 151n8

Blackness: Bible and, 39, 63; death associated with, 28; as evil, 131n1; Goldenberg's text finding on, 42, 138n11; lower class linkage with, 54; Middle Ages art and, 43; praise of, 29, 134n24; slavery basis in discourse on Bible figures, 63

Blemmye, 97, 103

Bloch, R. Howard, 53, 134n24

Blood, purity of, 2

Blumenbach, Johann Friedrich, 9–10, 128nn6–7, 131n41

Boccaccio, Giovanni, 5, 44, 59–62

Bodel, Jean, 79

Boulle, Pierre H., 26, 132n6

Calin, William, 148n71

Campbell, Kofi Omoniyi Sylvanus, 28, 29

Canada, Cartier's travels to, 104–5, *106*, *107*

Candace, 61–62

Cartier, Jacques, 104–5, *106*, *107*

Cassenti, Frank, 112, 118–25, 151nn9–10, 151nn13–16

Caste system, in Irving's *Alhambra*, 16

Casting practices, 112–13, 150n4

Catholic Bible, 137n10

Chanson de Guillaume, 84, 85, 147n68

Chanson de Roland, 10, 74, 80, 119, 121, 130n32; Cassenti's film, 118–25, 151nn9–10, 151nn13–16

Charlemagne, 79, 118–22, 125

Chartres Cathedral, 54, *55*

Chaucer, 82–84, 147nn65–66

Chevalerie Vivien, 85

Children, women's role in traits of, 65. *See also* Mixed-race children

Christian, Saracen, and Genre in Medieval French Literature (Ramey), 135n39

Christianity: culture construction, 34; Mongol influence on, 33–34

Christian-Muslim interactions: literary overview, 1–2. *See also specific texts*

Christians: early artists' portrayal of Muslims and, 74, 145n47; Gothic, 3–4, 11, 14–16, 22, 130, 130n27; reproduction battles between pagans and, 67; Saracen unions with, 85–86

The Chronicles of Moses, 40

Cinema, Middle Ages representations in: medieval cinema term, 150n6; 1970s French, 122; racial tolerance depiction, 111–18; racism depiction, 118–22

City of God (*De Civitate Dei*) (Augustine of Hippo), 91, 93

City of Ladies (Pizan), 59–62

Clapp, Nicholas, 46–47

Class, 8, 26, 28, 38; blackness linked with lower, 54; in cinema representations of Middle Ages, 114–15, 117, 121, 123–25; in Irving's Spain, 13, 16; miscegenation and, 66–67; race and, 13, 16

Climate theory, 52–53, 94

Colonization: culture of hybridity theory of race and, 31–32, 135n39; dominant-dominated discourse on, 33–35; medieval literature as grounding, 5–6; racial inferiority grounding, 28; slavery replacing onus of conversion, 109

Columbus, Christopher, 5, 12, 89, 103–4, 148n4

Commentaries, twelfth and thirteenth-century evolution of, 51

Congolese Observatory of Human Rights, 109

Conversion, religious: forced, 79; gender role in, 78–82; by logic, 78–79, 82; in medieval race conceptions, 31, 32, 36–37; onus of, 109; in romantic literature, 32, 135n39; taint and, 36, 78–82. *See also specific texts*

Convivencia, 16–17, 31–32

Cosa, Juan de la, 103

Criminals, Lombroso's study of skulls of, 36–37

Crosses, New World explorers use of, 90, 148n2

Crusades, 31, 33, 113–14, 119, 125; crusader kingdoms, 87, 135n39, 135n42, 136n2

Culture: assimilation in romance literature, 86–87, 149n71; Crusader kingdoms sharing of, 136n2; cultural traits and racism, 133n13; culture sharing in Bible, 136n2; dominator-dominated relations construction of, 33–35; of hybridity, 31–32, 135n39

Curse of Ham, 39, 42–44, *43*, 102, 137n10, 138n11

Cushites, 41, 137n9

Cuvier, Georges, 18

Cynocephali, 95, 98–99, *99*, 101, 103

Les damnés de la terre (*The Wretched of the Earth*) (Fanon), 124

Dante, 91

Darley, F.O.C., 14, *15*, 130nn26–27

Darwin, Charles, 18

Dasyus, *20, 21*, 23–24

Daughters of the American Revolution, 11

Dayan, Colin, 29, 30, 31

De animalibus (Magnus), 94–95

De arca Noe mistica (*On the mystical interpretation of Noah's Ark*) (Hugh of Saint-Victor), 96–97

Death, black association with, 28

De Civitate Dei (*City of God*) (Augustine of Hippo), 91, 93

De Generis Humani Varietate Nativa (*On the Natural Varieties of Mankind*) (Blumenbach), 9

De Gobineau, Arthur, 23

Delacampagne, Christian, 27, 132n3, 133n13

Delécluze, Étienne-Jean, 18

De proprietatibus rerum (*On the Properties of Things*) (Bartholomaeus), 28, 97

Desceliers, Pierre, 105, *106, 107*

De Weever, Jacqueline, 62, 135n34

Dinshaw, Carolyn, 147n66

Dogs: cynocephali, 95, 98–99, *99*, 101, 103; Muslims as represented by, 70, 143n23

Dominant-dominated discourse, 33–35

Douay-Rheims Bible, 44–45, 137n3, 137n10

D'Souza, Dinesh, 113

Eleanor of Aquitaine, 35

Emery, Elizabeth, 7

Enlightenment era, 11

Essai de poétique médiévale (Zumthor), 122

Essai sur l'inégalité des races humaines (*The Inequality of Human Races*) (De Gobineau), 23

"Esthétique appliquée à l'histoire de l'art" (Viollet-le-Duc), 23–24

Ethiopians, 28; Cushites and, 41, 137n9; Ethiopian bride of Moses, 39–42, *41*, 137nn3–4, 137n9; queen Nicaula, 59, 60, 61–62

Ethnicity, in race definitions, 25

Ethnocentrism, 132n8

Etymologiae (*Etymologies*) (Isidore of Seville), 66–67, 94

Evans, E. P., 134n28

Eve-Mary dichotomy, 53, 62

Explorers. *See* New World

Fanon, Frantz, 124

Ferrante, Joan, 59–60

Fille du comte de Pontieu, 71–74, 77, 80, 82, 143nn31–32, 144nn33–38, 145nn39–42; two versions of, 72, 143n28

Films. *See* Cinema, Middle Ages representations in

Finke, Laurie A., 151n8
First Persian Gulf War, 114
Flores, Ángel, 8
Fouchet, Max-Pol, 17
France: Cassenti's, 123–25; Communist
Party of, 123; Muslims in 1970s, 122–23;
succession rights in thirteenth-century,
34. *See also* New World
Fredrickson, George M., 127n8, 132n4,
132n8
Freedman, Paul, 28
Freeman, Morgan, 113–14
French cinema, 1970s, 122
French literature, medieval, 135n39;
Christian-Muslim interactions in,
1–2; Saracen princesses of, 54. *See also*
Fille du comte de Pontieu; Guillaume
d'Orange epic cycle; *Song of Roland*
French medievalists, nineteenth-century
premier, 130n32
Friedman, John Block, 143n23
Furness, Frank, 131n36

Galen, 66, 74, 141n5
Garden of Eden, 96–97
Gender: conversion role of, 78–82; inheri-
tance laws and, 35–36; lineage traced
through, 34–35
Gender-race intersection, 28–29, 31,
62–63, 135n34; man and white catego-
ries in, 77
Genealogical thinking, 10–11
Generation of Animals (Aristotle), 65
Genetics, 1, 5, 34–35, 64, 128, 132nn2–4
Gerard of Cremona, 141n5
"La geste que Turoldus declinet," 118–22,
151n12
Gilbert, Jane, 68–69, 143n26
Glacken, Clarence J., 131n1
Golden Age, medieval race and, 111–25
Goldenberg, David, 42, 127n4, 138n11
Gothic Christians, 3–4, 11, 14–16, 22, 130,
130n27
Gothic-Moor miscegenation, 16–17
Grail, 76–77, 78, 147n64

Great Chain of Being, 91, 92, 148n5
Great Khan, 102
Greeks, 131n38; Viollet-le-Duc's protagonists, 19, 20, 22
Guillaume d'Orange epic cycle, 32, 80,
84–87, 144n38, 147n62, 147nn68–69,
148nn70–71; Christian-Saracen unions
and conversions, 85–86

The Habitations of Man in All Ages (*His-
toire de l'habitation humaine*) (Viollet-
le-Duc), 19
Halter, Marek, *41*, 41–42
Ham, curse of, 39, 42–44, *43*, 63, 102,
137n10, 138n11
Harrison, Rex, 113
Hearn, M. F., 131n36
Hebrew Bible, 49, 139n30
Heng, Geraldine, 28–29, 37–38, 131n1,
134n21, 147n66; on alienness and con-
version, 84
Heredity, 26, 65, 66, 68, 82, 89
Hernstein, Richard J., 113
Hippocrates, 74, 77
Hippolytus of Rome, 57
Hispano-Umayyad rulers, 34–35
Histoire de l'habitation humaine (*The
Habitations of Man in All Ages*) (Viollet-
le-Duc), 19, *20*, *20–21*, 22, 23
History of the Mongols (John of Plano
Carpini), 33–34
Hochelaga, 105, *107*
Hugh of Saint-Victor, 96–97, 98, 104
Humanness, 29–32, 134nn27–28, 134n30;
animal-human creatures, *100*, 101, 103;
Augustine on, 91, 93; Isidore's view
of, 94; of Jews, 30; modern era debate
over, 102–10; Plinian races in debate
over, 90–91, 93; of pygmies, 94–95;
universalism view of, 91
Hunt, Tony, 148n71
Hybridity: animal-human, *100*, 101, 103;
animal-plant, 65–66, *100*, 101; cultural
and racial, 31–32, 135n39; religious, 32,
135n39; romance literature, 86–87

Medieval period. *See* Middle Ages; *specific topics*

Medieval race, 25–38; anti-Semitism in, 135n34; conversion in, 31, 36–37; Dayan's thinglikeness, 30, 31, 54; gender and, 28–29, 31, 62–63, 135n34; Golden Age and, 111–25; hybridity and, 135n39; praise of black skin as prejudice in, 29, 134n24; racism in cinematic representations, 118–22; skin color significance, 25, 28, 131n1, 132n4, 134n21. *See also* Bible; Literature, medieval

Medieval studies: on anti-Semitism, 127n1; Irving's influence on formation of, 7, 8–17; nationalism and, 4, 7–8, 17, 127n2

Melon-lambs, *100*, 101

Memmi, Albert, 132n3

Middle Ages: Age of Discovery continuities with, 89–90, 148n4; artwork, 43; Bible used most in, 137n10; Christian-Muslim interactions in, 1–2; cinematic representations of, 111–22; conversion in, 31; Irving's influence on modern perceptions of, 8–17, 129n13; medical science in, 64–65; modern era rupture with, 4, 27, 37, 133n12; need for expanded view of, 3; pivotal moments in, 3; Renaissance disconnect with, 136n54; Viollet-le-Duc's perceptions of, 17–24. *See also specific topics*

Mimicry, 31, 32

Miramon, Charles de, 26

Miscegenation: class and, 66–67; Gothic-Moor, 16–17; Irving's view of, 11, 14–16, 130n28; in literary imagination, 64–88; modern era and, 118; skin color and, 64; tales of thwarted, 82–87. *See also* Romance literature; *specific texts*

Misogyny, medieval, 53, 134n24; anti-Semitism and, 1, 31; Pizan's response to Boccaccio's, 59–62

Mixed-race children, 14, 35, 37, 47, 64; inherited traits and, 65; monstrous offspring, 65–71, 142n10, 143n26; in

romance literature, 76–78, 87. *See also specific texts*

Modern era: early, 37, 102–10; human-ness debate in early, 102–10; medieval miscegenation and, 118; Middle Ages disconnect from, 4, 27, 37, 133n12; modernists, 3

Monastery of idolators, 98, 99

Mongols, 9–10, 33–34, 136n47

Moniage Rainouart, 32, 84, 86

Monstrous races: Augustine on human-ness of, 91, 93; cynocephali, 95, 98–99, *99*; early modern encounters, 102–10; in Great Chain of Being, 91, 92, 148n5; Mandeville's accounts of, *100*, 101–2; monstrous offspring, 65–71, 142n10, 143n26; New World peoples as, 89–90; Plinian races as, 90–91, 93, 94, 97; salvation and, 91, 93, 96; troglodytes, 30, 97, 103, 105

Moore, Megan, 139n23

Moors, 16–17, 113–14, 130n27. *See also specific texts*

Morality, skin color and, 70, 74

Morgan, Edmund S., 148n4

Morowitz, Laura, 7

Moses, Ethiopian bride of, 39–42, *41*, 137nn3–4, 137n9

Mouvance, 122

Muldoon, James, 131n1

Multiculturalism, 148n71; in cinema, 113–14

Muslims: Abencerrages, 14, 16; in Cas-senti's film, 119–21; dogs as represent-ing, 70, 143n23; early artists' portrayal of Christians and, 74, 145n47; Middle Ages influence on modern views of, 1–2; moral inferiority view of, 74; in 1970s France, 122–23; racial profiling of, 36. *See also specific literary texts*

Nationalism, 4, 7–8, 17, 127n2

Natural History (Pliny), 90–91, 93

Nazi regime, 131n41

Neoplatonism, 51, 53
Nepaulsingh, Colbert, 27, 28
New Spain, 108
New World: crosses used to mark discovery, 90, 148n2; explorers, 5–6, 89–90, 96–97, 103–10, *106*, *107*, 148n2, 149n18; indigenous people of, 104–5, *106*, *107*, 108–10; Renaissance travelers view of, 89–90. *See also* Age of Discovery
Nicaula (queen of Ethiopia), 59, 60, 61–62
Nicholas of Lyra, 52–53, *57*, 59
Nigra sum, 50, 52–53
Nilus, 48–49
Noah, 94, 102
Non-Traditional Casting Project (NTCP), 112
Northumbria, 82–83, 147n66
NTCP. *See* Non-Traditional Casting Project

Odoric of Pordenone, 98–99, *99*, *100*, 101
Old Christians (viejos cristianos), 16
One-seed theory, 65–66, 68, 69–70, 81–82
On Famous Women (Nicholas of Lyra), *57*, 59
On the mystical interpretation of Noah's Ark (De arca Noe mistica) (Hugh of Saint-Victor), 96–97
On the Natural Varieties of Mankind (De Generis Humani Varietate Nativa) (Blumenbach), 9–10
On the Origin of Species (Darwin), 18
On the Properties of Things (De proprietatibus rerum) (Bartholomaeus), 28, 97
Orientalism (Said), 2
Origen of Alexandria, 47–48, 51, 53, 139n27, 140n36
Outlaw, Lucius, 128n9, 131n1
Oxford, *Song of Roland* of, 119, 120

Pacific Fur Company, 11
Pagans, 31, 39, 60, 61, 67; Northumbrian, 82–83, 147n66. *See also* Sheba

Pangenesis, 66, 74
Paris, Gaston, 130n32
Parzival (Wolfram), 32, 74–78, 146nn48–49, 146nn51–57
Peter of Auvergne, 95
Peter the Venerable, 30, 78
Petrarch, 3
Pizan, Christine de, 5, 44, 59–62
Plants, hybridity in animals and, 65–66
Plato, 51, 52, 53
Pliny the Elder, 90–91, 93, 94, 97, 101
Positive racism, Memmi's, 132n3
Praise, of black skin, 29, 134n24
Presentism, 133n10
Prise d'Orange, 84, 148n71
Prophets, Pizan's women, 60–61
Proto-racial society, 2, 127n3
Purity of blood, 2
Pygmies, 26, 29, 94–95, 101, *106*; treatment of contemporary, 109

Quayle, Dan, 116
Queens. *See* Belacane; Nicaula; Sheba

Rabelais, François, 89–90
Race: architecture link with, 18–24; Blumenbach's treatise on, 9–10, 128n6, 131n41; class and, 13, 16; climate theory of, 52–53; definition of, 25, 132n2; evolution of term, 26–27; moment of, 33; Outlaw's theories of, 128n9, 131n1; proto-racial society, 2, 127n3; racism distinguished from, 25–26; Semitic, 10, 131n41. *See also* Bible; Medieval race; *specific literary works; specific topics*
"Race or Culture: Medieval Notions of Difference" (Muldoon), 131n1
Race theories: Blumenbach's, 9–10, 128nn6–7; Heng on Middle Ages importance in, 37–38; history of, 26–28, 37–38, 128nn8–9; postcolonial, 31, 32; thinglikeness, 30, 31, 54. *See also* Medieval race

Racism: Appiah on, 133n13; cinematic representations of medieval, 118–22; cultural traits and, 133n13; definitions of, 25, 132n3, 132n8, 133n13; Fredrickson's ethnocentrism in defining, 132n8; 9/11 racial profiling, 36; positive, 132n3; praise of blackness as, 29, 134n24; race distinguished from, 25–26

Rainouart (literary figure), 32, 36, 84, 85–86

Ramey, Lynn Tarte, 135n39

Rationality, 93, 101

Reason, Magnus on, 94–95

Reis, Piri, 103–4

Religion: as central to Middle Age questions of difference, 36; heredity and, 82; hybrid, 32, 135n39; skin color as indicating, 36. See also Conversion, religious

Renaissance: explorers, 104–5, 106, 107, 108–10; line between Middle Ages and, 136n54; maps, 102; Middle Age viewed by thinkers of, 3; monstrous races view of New World peoples, 89–90

Reproduction, 64; battle of, 67; conversion and, 71; Hippocratic model of, 74, 77; Isidore's theory of, 66–67; judicium dei model of, 67, 71, 74, 77, 141n8; monstrous offspring, 65–71, 142n10, 143n26; one-seed theory of, 65–66, 68, 69–70, 81–82; pangenesis view of, 66, 74; sexual transformations, 70, 141n2; two-seed model of, 66, 67, 77

Revue des cours littéraires de la France et de l'étranger, 18

Reynolds, Kevin, 113, 114, 117, 125

Robin Hood: Prince of Thieves, 113–14, 117, 118, 150n7

Romance literature, 68–88; conversion in, 32, 135n39; cultural assimilation reading of, 86–87, 149n71; Fille du comte de Pontieu, 71–74, 80, 82, 143n28, 143nn31–32, 144nn33–38, 145nn39–42; as hybrid genre, 86–87; mixed-race children in,

76–78, 87; Parzival, 32, 74–78, 146nn48–49, 146nn51–57; racial consciousness in, 87–88. See also Guillaume d'Orange epic cycle

Romeo and Juliet, 112–13

Ruggles, D. Fairchild, 34–35

Saartjie. See Baartman, Sara

Saguenay (mythical land), 104

Said, Edward, 2

Saladin, 73

Salimbene of Parma, 97

Salvation, 53, 63; East-West movement of, 96, 104; Eve-Mary dichotomy and, 50; in mapping framework, 96–97; monstrous races and, 91, 93, 96; onus of, 96–97, 149n18; women's role in, 51

Saracens, 22, 35, 135n39; Agareni as, 53; defined, 136n1; Grail guardians and, 147n64; whitening of princesses, 54. See also Fille du comte de Pontieu; The King of Tars

Science, nineteenth-century, 17

Scientific racism, 7–8, 24, 37

Scraba, Jeffrey, 129n13

Semitic race, 10, 131n41

Septuagint, 49

Sepúlveda, Juan Ginés de, 103–4

Sexual transformations, 70, 77, 141n2

Shakespeare, William, 89–90, 112–13

Sheba (queen), 45–47, 138nn16–17, 138n19, 139n23; Kebra Nagast version of, 46, 138n20; Nicaula and, 60; Nicholas of Lyra on, 59; other names for, 44; westernized depictions of, 54, 55–58, 59; whitening of, 48, 64; in works of Boccaccio and Pizan, 59–62. See also Song of Songs

Shem, 102

Shichtman, Martin B., 151n8

Sketch Book (Irving), 9

Skin color: colonization and, 31; magpie comparison, 76; medieval literature descriptions not detailing, 73–74; medieval race defined by, 25, 28, 131n1, 132n4, 134n21; miscegenation and, 64; morality linked with, 70, 74; Nicholas of Lyra on origins of, 53; religion indicated by, 36. *See also* Blackness; Literature, medieval; *specific texts*

Slavery, 6, 25–26, 29, 63, 108–9

Snowden, Frank M., Jr., 127n4, 131n1

Solomon. *See* Sheba; Song of Songs

Song of Roland, 39, 119, 120

The Song of Roland (film), 111

Song of Songs (Song of Solomon), 45, 47–63, 55–58; Aristotelian commentaries on, 52; Augustinian principles applied to, 51; commentaries as metaphorical, 135n34; commentary consistencies, 54; early commentaries on, 47–51; in Hebrew and English Bible translations, 49, 139n30; "I am black *and* beautiful" and "I am black *but* beautiful," 49, 50, 54, 139n30; literal and anagogical, metaphorical readings of, 52; Sheba addressing Jewish women in, 48–49; twelfth and thirteenth-century commentaries on, 51–54; women, Jews and blacks linkage, 52, 53, 69; women treated in modern studies compared with medieval, 140n41. *See also* Black Bride; *specific commentators*

Spain: fifteenth-century "purity of blood" concept in, 2; Irving's history of, 8–17, 129n13; New, 108; tourism centered on Moors of, 16; Visigoths, 129n15. *See also* New World

Speculum historiale (Vincent of Beauvais), 34

The Spell-Bound Gateway, 15

Steel, Karl, 134n27

Succession crisis, of rulers, 34–36; in romance literature, 71, 72–73, 76–77, 80–81, 85

Summerson, John, 131n35

Synagogue, black bride as, 47

Syria, 84

Taint, 36, 78–82

Talmud, 138n11

The Tempest (Shakespeare), 89–90

Thinglikeness, Dayan's, 30, 31, 54

Tiers Livre (Rabelais), 89–90

Toler, Pamela, 130n28

T-O maps, 27, 44, 96, *107*

"Toward a Critical Theory of 'Race'" (Outlaw), 128n9

Tower of Babel, 94, 102, 149n8

Traces on the Rhodian Shore (Glacken), 131n1

Translatio studii (transfer of knowledge), 19, 131n38

Travels (Mandeville), 101–2

Travel writing, 33

Troglodytes, 30, 97, 103, 105

Turoldus, 118–22, 151n12

Two-seed model, 66, 67, 77

Umayyad rulers, Hispano-, 34–35

Unicorns, 105, *106*

United States, Irving's view on origins of, 11

Universalism, humanness and, 91

Viejos cristianos (old Christians), 16

Vincent of Beauvais, 34

Viollet-le-Duc, Eugène-Emmanuel, 18–24, *20, 21*, 131nn35–36, 131n41; medieval architecture restorations by, 17–18

Virgin, 134n24

Visigoths, 129n15

Voyage of St. Brendan, 43

Walker Bynum, Caroline, 140n42

Whitaker, Cord, 147nn65–66

Whitening, 48–49, 54, 63, 64

Wolfram von Eschenbach, 32, 74–78. *See also Parzival*

Women: child's traits role of, 65; Eve-Mary dichotomy, 53, 62; as gifts between men, 47, 63, 139n23; misogyny, 1, 31, 53, 59–61, 134n24; religious conversion for, 80;

Women—*continued*
    salvation role of, 51; Saracen, 35; Sheba
    story's Jewish, 48–49, 52, 53, 69; Song of
    Songs medieval-modern comparison,
    140n41
The Wretched of the Earth (*Les damnés de
    la terre*) (Fanton), 124

Wright, Frank Lloyd, 131n36

Ydolatras (idol worshipers), 103

Zazamanc, Moorish queen of, 32, 74–76
Zipporah (Halter), *41*, 41–42
Zumthor, Paul, 122

LYNN RAMEY is associate professor of French and resident scholar in the Center for Second Language Studies at Vanderbilt University. She is the author of *Christian, Saracen and Genre in Medieval French Literature* and the coeditor of *Race, Class, and Gender in "Medieval" Cinema*.

৩৭

CPSIA information can be obtained
at www.ICGtesting.com
Printed in the USA
BVHW030713080121
597230BV00007B/207